SIDE-WAYS to the SUN

SIDE-WAYS to the SUN

a novel by
Linda Sillitoe

SIGNATURE BOOKS
SALT LAKE CITY, UTAH
1987

AUTHOR'S NOTE: "The genesis for this story occurred in a newspaper city room, the busy resting place of thousands of unwritten tales. However, the unfolding events and the characters portrayed here are entirely fictional, making any resemblance to actual persons or situations wholly coincidental."

Book and cover design by Connie Disney.
Cover illustration by Rob Blackard.

Library of Congress Cataloging-in-Publication Data

Sillitoe, Linda, 1948–
        Sideways to the sun.

        I. Title.
PS3569.I447S5   1987   813'.54   86-4463
ISBN 0-941214-56-7

For my enablers —
John, Melissa, Robbie, and Cynthia

CONTENTS

1

MEGAN

Megan watched morning paint her picture window violet then mauve. She considered the fact that this was the first time she had seen this happen without a sick child on her lap. Scott, at two, for instance, breathing like a tuneless pipe organ despite her efforts to steam loose the croup. Or Elinor, at nine months, twitching at the peak of a chicken pox fever when her nervous system set off alarms everywhere.

Never before tonight and last night had Megan sat up waiting for her husband, Richard.

When the window finally turned gray, Megan shifted in the chair. The dark lump of the telephone reminded her to call. The police sergeant had told her the afternoon paper in Salt Lake City would be running a full shift by 6 a.m. It must be nearly that now. Still she hesitated.

First she must assure herself that this would be easier than the morning calls yesterday when she'd telephoned Richard's boss and finally the Salt Lake City Police Department. Richard worked in Salt Lake.

The thought of Richard leaving for work each morning and returning each night all their seventeen years of married life almost produced the jangle of his keys in the lock and the thump of his shoulder against the door that always stuck until mid-April. But when she let out her breath and drew another, ears straining, she knew no one was there. There had been no one all night or all last night. Richard never stayed out all night. He called if he'd be so much as half an hour late.

Megan was amazed to still be alive after two nights of crisis. She wasn't the type for traumatic situations. Her hands fidgeted along the seams of the slacks she'd put on Monday morning, not knowing she'd forget to change them for two days. She'd managed well the evening before, sending Nancy home to her family next door after Dale Brown, the bishop, left. "Maybe I'll doze if I'm alone," she told Nancy. "Anyway, there's nothing you can do."

But there had been no sleeping, no thinking really, just one jolt of emotion after another. Anger seared her, drowned by guilt for being angry. Then it was all swept away by relief. If she could feel anger toward Richard, he must be all right. Impossibly inconsiderate, yes, taking revenge for some wrong she could not even imagine, but all right.

All right meant her world had not disintegrated, that he was coming back.

Fear trickled like acid into her stomach. She knew Richard so well. He'd never let her endure this anguish if he could prevent it.

He must be sick or hurt or amnesic. Or murdered, his body lying by a canyon road as other bodies had, names in the newspaper, faintly shady statistics without substance.

Megan had to switch on a lamp so she could see the number she'd jotted down. Outside, street lights highlighted bits of trim and railing on the invisible houses opposite her. Here came morning up the hill.

"This is the *Deseret News*, may I help you?" It was a woman's voice.

"Yes," Megan cleared her throat. "I need to talk to someone about a missing person. The police said I should give information to the newspapers so you can run his description and photograph."

There was a pause. "This is a missing person?"

"Yes. My husband is . . . missing."

"Well, I don't think we usually . . . I'll tell you what," she began again after skipping a beat as Megan's throat tightened. "You give me the information and I'll see what I can do."

"All right. I can bring a photograph to you later this morning."

"Okay. I'll check on that, too. How long has your husband been missing?"

"Since Monday morning when he left for work." Why, Megan thought, didn't I *see* him when he left? Why did it take going through his closet to find out which shirt he wore?

"Monday morning." Megan had the idea the woman was typing, but she couldn't hear a machine. "And this is Wednesday morning. Did he arrive at work?"

"Yes. His supervisor told me when I called yesterday that Richard came into his office about nine Monday morning and said that he didn't feel well. His supervisor sent him home. He said Richard looked pale and shaky, so he walked him to the elevator. That's the last we know of him."

"Mmmm. Okay. What does he look like?"

"He's five feet ten inches, about 160 pounds, light blond hair cut fairly short, medium build, blue eyes. That day he wore a blue shirt with dark blue pinstripes, navy slacks, black shoes, and a blue tweed sport coat."

There was a pause. Megan added, "That's one reason it's so strange. He just had that sport coat. It still gets so cold at night, and if he's sick and wandering . . . " She stopped and swallowed hard, then the words rushed out again. "Also, maybe you should know he's a very responsible person. We have four young children, and he's the Elders' Quorum president in our Mormon ward, and he's always been very reliable." She pressed her knuckles against her mouth.

"Okay." The voice sounded sympathetic. "Did he have anything with him that day?"

"Yes, a small attache case. He's a legislative researcher for the state."

"Okay. And you said you've contacted the police?"

"Yes. I called the Bountiful police, since that's where we live. Then I had to call the Salt Lake police, since that's where he was last seen. I think there's been a breakdown in communication or something. No one in either department seems to be doing much."

"I guess you checked your bank accounts?" The voice turned apologetic.

"He has no money," Megan replied flatly. "A few dollars, of course, but not much. The police checked that right away. And he has no valuable rings or anything like that."

"Okay. Can you hold on just a minute?"

Megan heard the receiver rap against something hard, and vague office noises filled her ear. In a few seconds she heard the reporter's voice, then a male voice overriding it loudly enough for Megan to catch some of the words.

" . . . don't run it. Almost always, these guys are runaways . . . " Megan took a deep breath. As soon as she let it go, she heard the woman again, talking emphatically.

" . . . but four children, reliable . . . he has no money with him . . . " Then the man's voice cut in and Megan closed her eyes and tried to stop hearing. When the woman came back on line, Megan eased the pressure of the telephone against her ear.

"Hello?"

"Yes, I'm here."

"I spoke to our city editor. I'm going to give this information to our Davis County Bureau. If something shows up in the Salt Lake police reports, we'll get it from our beat reporter." Megan listened hard, trying to sort out the jargon, but all she heard was no. A placating note was in the voice now, something Megan was beginning to recognize.

"What about the photograph?"

"I'll make a note of that. If you hear any more, you might call the Davis Bureau."

Megan wrote down the number and hung up. So. Richard had disappeared and it wasn't news. Evidently it happened all the time. Still, she found some comfort in the reporter taking her part against the editor. She switched off the lamp before Nancy saw it and hurried over. All up and down the street, the houses sat as placid and fat as cows in a pasture. Bountiful was known for its stability, its rows of lovely homes and green yards, and its blond children. A bedroom to Salt Lake, it was plusher than most.

When Richard and the real estate agent drove her to see this house just before Scott was born, she'd misread the sign as Storybook Lane. It was Stonybrook.

The street looked so calm in the morning light that it both comforted and mocked her. She turned away.

"I'm afraid," she found herself whispering to Richard's fish in the aquarium. The large, black goldfish stared through the glass.

Megan stood up stiffly, went to the aquarium, and took out the fish food in the cupboard below.

She watched the fish mouth its way from speck to speck, some of the others starting to follow. Then she went down the hall to the bathroom, turned on the light, and closed the door.

When she stared into the mirror while washing her hands, she saw that her dark hair had not turned white.

Raven, Richard used to call her, running his hand down the cropped back of her hair. "Why didn't they name you Raven instead of Megan?" Even now her hair was only slightly mussed. Her lipstick, drawn last evening for the children and the bishop's sake, edged her lips with orange-colored flakes. She bit them away. Dark stains bordered her eyes above and below, but their hazel centers looked back at her steadily beneath the straight, dark brows.

The warm water spraying over her hands made her long for a hot shower. Why hadn't she taken one sometime in this endless night? Now the alarm clock would be ringing down the hall in Becky's room. Were there enough bananas and chips for the kids' lunches? Richard usually ran to the store in the evening when the supply of lunch stuff dwindled, as it always did mid-week.

Megan decided she'd shower after the children left for school — if no word had come.

There was a knock at the bathroom door and Megan jumped, her hand flying to her throat. "Come in," she managed.

The door flew open and Becky glared at her. With her hair tangled and her lower lip out, she looked younger than her almost-sixteen years, more like the stormy little girl Megan still missed sometimes. "I slept!"

"That's all right. You needed sleep."

"Well, so do you."

"I can get a nap later. You have to go to school."

"How can I concentrate? Why don't I stay home and help you?"

"No." A headache began at the base of Megan's skull

like a mushroom breaking the earth. "Really, it's more help
to know you're all busy and not worrying too much."

At that, Becky's tears erupted. "Mother, we worry
in the cafeteria. In the orchestra. Yesterday I went to the
restroom after first period and just cried."

Megan gathered her into her arms and let her weep,
wondering if it was sleep that gave her the strength to cry.
Megan felt battered but bloodless. Even morning sickness
didn't register now, maybe because she hadn't had any sleep.

"Wash your face, honey. I've got to go wake Scott."
Scott was still in junior high, but he usually left as early as
Becky and finished his homework at school.

Walking down the hall, Megan wondered if Richard
had ever done anything so difficult as waking their children
to another day of his absence. But again guilt overcame her.
Right now Richard might be enduring ropes and a gag,
worrying about their fears. Or a terrible blankness might
have erased his knowledge of them, leaving him a vagrant
because he couldn't remember home.

Scott came awake at once, staring at her from eyes
shaped exactly like Richard's. "Is he back?"

"No, not yet. Come and get some breakfast, then
get dressed. I'll start the lunches."

She couldn't say more, but she bent and kissed him
quickly. She heard him get out of bed as she walked away.
Today he would consider himself the man of the house.
Last night the bishop had shaken his hand and said, "I'm
counting on you to take care of things while your Dad's
gone." His man-to-man tone was quite different from the
soothing syrup he poured on Megan's ears. Scott had nod-

ded seriously as Megan smiled at him. Then she'd looked down at her empty hands.

Two bananas, one in each lunch box, two bags of chips, two small cans of tomato juice, four slices of white bread slicked with mayonnaise, two slices of cheese, ham for Becky, dried beef for Scott. Elinor would take school lunch.

When reading of disasters or hearing about friends' problems, Megan had always assumed that older children were a great comfort in a crisis and accepted responsibility almost automatically. Now she began to wonder if her little girls, only ten and four years old, would emerge from this crisis the least hurt. Or did they only show it less? As Megan worked and wondered, Becky and Scott wordlessly ate their cereal and drank their milk, then left to get dressed.

A stroke, Megan thought. Richard had been so quiet and tense lately. Maybe he had high blood pressure. With a stroke he might be unable to speak. Still, a look in his wallet would tell his name, his address, even his insurance number.

But he'd been on the bus. What if someone took his wallet and left the bus? Then, angry and frustrated, Richard strode down the aisle and the stroke hit. She could see his knees buckle toward the unreliable floor, his body tilt toward the steel posts that run to the ceiling, the side of his head swinging into the pole as he slumped . . .

"Mother."

Megan spun to find Elinor twisting her long, almost-white braid with both hands. "I've got to call the bus company," Megan told her.

"You called them yesterday."

"Did I? Oh, yes, I did." Elinor still gazed at her from improbably blue eyes. Megan knelt on the floor beside her and felt Elinor's arms circle her neck. Still the child said nothing.

"Daddy's not home yet, Elinor."

"I noticed that." Megan kissed her temple where short hairs sprang into curls.

"Well, come and get some breakfast."

"I never eat when a member of the family is a missing person." She turned on her heel and left the room.

Megan shook her head. Maybe some chocolate milk and a granola bar would tempt her after the older children left. What was it she'd said? She'd have to remember to tell Rich . . .

"Your slip shows," she said to Becky, who'd hurried in with her arms full of books and now looked insulted. She softened her tone. "Here, let me help you. You always look so pretty in blue."

"Mom?"

"Yes, honey."

"You're pregnant, right?"

Megan's hands stopped at Becky's waist under the wool skirt. A pause before the question registered. "Yes, you know I am. Why?"

"It's just that . . . I mean . . . Dad would never leave, I mean he wouldn't *leave* for any reason. But I wanted to be sure he knows you're pregnant."

"Becky, of course he knows. And he wouldn't leave for any reason, you're right. Certainly not now."

"Then that means . . ."

Megan sighed sharply. What was worse? Thinking Richard had abandoned them without a word or that he was a victim?

Becky filled the silence. "Well, there's just got to be an explanation. Try to get some rest, Mom. And please make Elinor put back my black scarf! She's been parading around in it like a ghoul."

Scott gave Megan a long look as he picked up his lunch box and a quick hug before he strode out the door. He was like Richard. Whatever he felt was for her to surmise and for him to endure.

When Megan brought Elinor a cup of hot chocolate and a granola bar, she found her ready for school but sitting cross-legged on the foot of Heather's bed. "See the dust fairies?" she was asking her sister. "See how they dance in the sun? Try to watch just one at a time. It disappears when I blow. See?"

Heather blew too, then laughed. "Where do they go? Look, they're back."

"Nowhere," Elinor said. "I think they just turn sideways to the sun."

She took a sip of the chocolate but set the granola bar beside her on the bed.

"I want hot chocolate, too," Heather said, struggling out of the blankets.

"In a minute. Let me braid Elinor's hair so she can be on her way."

Elinor sipped as Megan brushed the long hair, then sectioned it into three shining strands and began to braid.

The notches between waves locked together, as if she was assembling a simple, symmetrical puzzle.

"Elinor says dirt is really fairies." Heather stared at Megan from under her dark bangs.

"Dust," Elinor corrected. She handed Heather her half-full cup.

"Take hot lunch today," Megan said.

"I told you." Elinor put on her jacket and pulled her braid to the outside. "If Daddy comes back, tell him I'm hungry and furious."

"Wait." Megan felt panic choke her as Elinor turned to leave. "Get dressed," she told Heather. "We're going to walk Elinor to school." Then she remembered the telephone always on the verge of ringing, the chance of a knock at the door.

"Don't worry, Mom," Elinor's voice floated back. "I'm pretty bulky."

Megan laughed.

With the children gone, the telephone began first, followed by the doorbell. Neighbors and ward members stood on the porch, casseroles and cakes in their outstretched hands. The bishop called, the Relief Society president, and Nancy. With her little girl in kindergarten and her baby asleep, Nancy came over to answer the telephone while Megan answered the door.

In the early afternoon, though, it was Megan who picked up the ringing telephone to find only silence. "Hello?" she said again. "*Hello?*" Then her heart hammered so violently in her throat that she could only stare and listen. Nancy ran across the living room and grabbed the receiver.

"Hello? Richard? Who is it?" she cried in a breath. Kidnapped, Megan thought. Richard, be careful.

But no one answered Nancy, either, except the dial tone. She held the receiver away from her head and shrugged. The tone hummed in Megan's head hours after her heart stopped pounding.

Later Megan remembered the shower. "Will you answer the phone and door? I think the children should see me in clean clothes and out of the rocking chair."

"Take your time," Nancy said with her usual cheer. "Heather's fine, and Benjy's probably going to sleep a while longer."

"Thanks." Megan wanted to hug her but couldn't quite. She smiled and fled.

Megan shed her blouse and slacks as the water rushed into the tub. She wished she could also shed the long, stuffy hours of fear. She unhooked her bra, raising her shoulders as the grip of the straps relaxed. It was not until she removed her white garments, which she'd first slipped on at barely eighteen when she and Richard married in the Salt Lake Temple, that she saw the few dried spots of blood.

Her hand touched her belly and she felt neglectful. She hadn't given the baby, who was only two and one half months formed, a second thought since Monday. She'd always felt her unborn babies safe only if they were foremost in her thoughts. It's stress, she told herself, stepping into the tub. I've got to start eating and sleeping. This has got to end.

The soap and hot water felt wonderful on her skin. Her muscles relaxed, and the ache across her shoulder blades eased. Through the washcloth, her hand followed the curves and hollows of her body with the same casual pleasure she found brushing Elinor's hair.

She leaned back, hooked the base of her skull on the top of the tub, closed her eyes, and let her thoughts run. The water was nearly tepid when she jerked awake, staring straight ahead. Richard looked back at her, his eyes intent behind the horn-rimmed glasses he had gotten recently. But even as she gasped, he was gone. She sat up and scooped water on to her face, letting it drip off coldly.

The dream was not a vision but a memory. She'd wakened early one morning to find him in bed with those glasses on, staring at her fixedly as she slept. "My gosh! What's wrong?" she'd stammered.

In a second, his gaze wavered and he said, "Nothing. I've been up for a while, but I decided to come back to bed until the house warms. I was just thinking."

Now when did that happen? Was it Monday morning? No. Monday morning she'd been groggy with the sick, dank sleep of early pregnancy. This had been on a weekend when the room was fairly light as she woke. Maybe the Sunday before. Maybe two weeks ago. How could anyone pay close enough attention?

When she toweled herself, she was relieved not to find any blood. Be all right, she sent to the baby inside her by the internal telepathy that had become familiar.

She brushed her teeth, combed her hair, and added light pink lipstick. She thought of smoothing makeup over the circles around her eyes but decided it would discolor them even more than they already were.

In fresh clothes she felt better and carried laundry

out with her. She could hear Nancy on the telephone rehears-
ing the same sparse facts. She began to sort the clothes,
then returned to the hamper for more.

By the time the first load of laundry was dry, Heather
was tucked under a blanket for her nap. Nancy and Benjamin
had gone home. When the dryer stopped, Megan hurried
through the silent house, opened the dryer door, and automatically began to fold the clothes.

She had folded at least four warm pairs of Richard's
cotton garments when her tears began. She folded a fifth
pair, letting the tears drip off her jaw, as if, ignored, they
would evaporate in their tracks. But more followed. Then a
shuddering began in her chest and deepened, rumbling into
the pit of her stomach, rising and bursting from her mouth
and nose. At last she sank on to the laundry room floor, the
stack of garments in her lap, and wept into their folds. Where
are you, she cried again and again. But she heard only her
own ragged breath. The garments she hugged absorbed her
tears from first to last with hardly a trace.

ELINOR

When Elinor came home from school she went into her room and shut the door. She always shut it, but Heather usually ran in and out, leaving the door open. Lately Heather wanted to be right in the same room with Mom, or, even better, on Mom's lap. That left Elinor in peace.

With the door shut, she could believe that Daddy had come home and that she just hadn't been told yet. It might be the first five minutes after he walked through the door. That would mean that any second a shout, a loud peal of laughter, something, could poof away the tension that filled the house like cigarette smoke — alien and despised. Mood had always fascinated Elinor, how it could change. Someone says something funny, Mom and Dad exchange a look or Heather makes a silly face. The world grows firm. Just a few words, like a spell.

Elinor was brushing her life size toy chimp's fur with a small hairbrush. She would need a long time to do the job right. She'd begun with his left foot, brushing the fur carefully over the plastic toes, which were rather like her own, so that it shone like dark silk. Poor Harry had been neglected for a long time, and his fur was crushed and matted.

"Boil, boil," she muttered, "toil and trouble." She and Cindy and Ginny were the witches in the class play. The teacher had given them a hard poem to memorize, and Elinor loved the sound of it. "Oh, Shakespeare," she could shrug, when someone asked what she was chanting. When her class had gone to the library today, she had found the whole play called MacBeth, but it was disappointingly hard to read. Better to take a short part and squeeze the music out in her mouth, she decided. Next time she would find another passage by Shakespeare.

She turned the chimp on its face and began brushing the back of one leg. She wanted to turn on the radio. Music would erase the voices outside her door, increasing the possibility that Daddy was home. But radios blared insistently in the living room and kitchen already, as if some answer would come between a linoleum commercial and the top ten tunes. She couldn't bear to bring that anticipation into her room, too. Someplace had to be safe.

Now, if she had black hair like Harry, she'd be perfect for the play. She could let it out of the braid and tangle it some, although it would hurt like the blazes to get it smooth again. With that dark, hairy screen around her face and a tooth blacked out with the wax Scott used last Halloween, she would be just right.

Monday she had told the teacher she would dye her hair black for the play. Cindy said a certain spray would wash right out. Miss Adams had shuddered. (Elinor had read that word "shuddered" often enough and tried to imagine how it looked. As soon as Miss Adams's head and shoulders twitched in that nervous way, Elinor felt a flash of recognition.)

"I don't know, Elinor," Miss Adams said doubtfully. "Your hair is so light. Promise me you won't put anything on it until you're sure it will wash out. And of course you've got to see what your mom says."

"Oh, she'll let me," Elinor said confidently.

"Maybe," Mom had actually said after school. "Tomorrow we'll go to the costume shops and see what they have. But we'll have to test it on one strand first. When is the play?"

Thursday, Elinor told her, you're invited. Now Thursday was tomorrow. And since Monday evening when Dad didn't come home for supper, or at bedtime, or ever, Mom hadn't mentioned the hair dye again. With Nancy and the bishop and the police stopping by, Elinor hadn't had the nerve to ask.

"Other leg, now," she told the chimp. "Maybe in Scotland all the witches were blond anyway. What do you think?"

When Elinor heard the front door shut, she froze, her brush hand lifted. She waited. There was no sound for perhaps four minutes. "Fire burn and cauldron bubble," she almost shouted.

Her door opened. It was Becky. "What?" Becky asked.

Elinor ignored her. Would she ask, "What?" if Dad had just come home?

"What did you say?" Becky tried again.

" 'Fire burn and cauldron bubble.' I was practicing for my play tomorrow."

"Well, it's nice to see someone who's not worried! Sister Johnson just brought us fried chicken for dinner. Come and eat."

Elinor kept brushing.

"Elinor! The last thing Mom needs is for you to act up."

Elinor could hear the tears under Becky's sarcasm, but she didn't care. Becky could be so unjust. She started brushing the fur on the chimp's bottom, the most matted, since he spent most of his time perched in her old rocking chair. The fur was smoothing out nicely, she thought.

"Hey!"

Now Scott was at the door. He watched her for a few minutes. "That's like splinting a giraffe's neck," he said finally. When she looked up he wrapped both hands around his neck, rolled his eyes up, and gargled like he was strangling.

Elinor managed a smile.

"You're probably too hefty to pull up," he said, holding out a hand. She took it, and he yanked, then kept her hand in his warm one maybe two extra seconds until they reached the door.

The table looked like Andy's Smorgasbord, Elinor thought, full of strange casseroles and salads she didn't know if she'd like. The old high chair in the corner caught her eye, and she looked at it instead. She could remember sitting there when she, not Heather, was the baby. She'd watch Daddy on Saturday mornings as he sang folk songs and flipped the French toast. Then, he liked to cook on Saturdays while Mom slept late.

Mom would always tease him when she came out in her duster, looking rosy and happy. "You always hated those folk songs when they were popular," she would say to him.

"Then all the songs wore beards," he would answer.

Elinor didn't know what he'd meant, but she liked the sound of it. She could imagine songs with beards and songs with flowing auburn hair and songs with punk cuts. But that memory made her feel like her stomach was a balloon — hollow but apt to pop if she put anything in.

"I have something to tell you," Mom was saying. Elinor looked up, surprised. Dinner was ending, not because their plates were empty, but because they were all tired of pretending to eat. Small scallops had been spooned from the edges of several dishes, Elinor noticed, and the tidy mounds still sat on their plates.

"We are all worried and scared and upset," Mom was saying. Elinor felt her ballooning stomach swell a little more. "But we are going to go on," she continued. Elinor watched her mother grab her water glass and drain it. Mom's throat must be hurting, too. Becky and Scott and Heather looked embarrassed and sulky. Elinor took a deep breath and wished for a burp.

"Heather," Mom was saying, "where were Mommy and Daddy married?"

"In the temple," Heather answered in her church voice. Elinor squirmed a little.

"That's right. And for how long?"

"Forever," Scott said.

"And what about you children? How long will you belong to me and to your Dad?"

"Forever," Becky said now. Elinor noticed her chin shaking. "As long as we're good," Becky added.

How good? Elinor wanted to ask.

Megan looked at Elinor and Elinor looked back. Elinor knew she wasn't likely to start Mom crying, but Becky was.

"That's right," she watched her mother say. "We don't know where Daddy is. We don't know why he isn't here or whether he's all right, and that's hard. But we do know that he belongs to us, and we still belong to him, too."

Elinor nodded. She saw the others nodding, as well.

But what did this mean? Elinor wondered. That they would just go on living like this, or would things get back to normal? Elinor waited until Heather and Scott stopped talking, then asked, "Mom, are you going to sit up all night again?"

She saw her mother look at the food on their plates, then move her hand against her own abdomen. "No," she said. "I'm going to bed tonight. Just like you."

Elinor nodded and picked up her fork.

"Becky's crying," Heather accused.

Elinor, sitting next to her mother, heard the long breath her mother took then. "Crying's okay," Mom said, adding, "and we'll each pick up our dishes."

They did, almost silently. Then Elinor took Heather's hand and they drifted around the house for a while, from room to room, until their mother told them to take their bath.

That night Elinor lay in her bed, awake long after Heather's breathing became regular, deep, and slow. She thought she could remember Monday morning when Dad left for work, even though she'd still been asleep in bed. She wasn't sure. The memory was so important. The police might think it was a clue. She could imagine herself on a big, wooden chair at some police station, her legs dangling. The somberness of that picture confused her thoughts.

All she knew was that when Dad didn't come home Monday night, she'd remembered Monday morning. She'd heard Daddy come whistling as he crossed the corner of the lawn by her room's big window, and she'd been sleepily surprised. Morning, she'd thought, Dad's going to work. His cheerfulness had made her happy as she swung her legs out of bed.

What should she do now? Tell Mom? Call the police? Tell Scott and Becky? But they wouldn't think it was important. "So he whistled?" she could already hear Scott say. "What does that prove?"

"That he likes us," Elinor wanted to reply. She said it to herself.

She sighed and fought tears down in her throat. Really, someone needed to cast a spell, something to bring him back safe, no questions asked. Of course, she had prayed already, again and again. They had all prayed, joining their hands in a circle. When they got up, they'd smiled at each

other with their wet faces. But a spell wouldn't hurt either.
She was a Girl Scout, now, not just a Brownie, and a scout
knew how important it was to be prepared in every possible
way.

She lay for a long time trying to make a spell. The
words jumbled in her head, but still she couldn't sleep.
Finally, she got up and tiptoed down the hall to Mom and
Dad's bedroom. When she passed the mirror on one double
door, she paused. In the dark, her navy nightgown was
invisible. Only her pale face and hair, her outstretched hands,
showed.

Her mother's gasp when Elinor stood quietly beside
the bed made Elinor jump. "I'm a witch, not a ghost," she
quickly explained.

Her mother made a small noise that might have been
a chuckle and opened the covers so that Elinor could come
inside. She felt her mother's face in the back of her hair, her
body curving around Elinor's. Then everything became warm
and still and safe again.

3

MEGAN

Megan dreamed that she and Richard were walking along the beach near San Diego. They were on their honeymoon, yet she knew everything that had happened in the nearly two decades since they married. Funny, but they felt like newlyweds again, awkward and raw together, yet bold, too, walking down the beach in their swimming suits.

Most of the time they'd worn shirts over their suits, worrying about sunburn, she remembered as her sleep lightened a little. Really, they wore shirts because they hadn't been comfortable nearly nude out there in daylight.

She could still hear the waves as she began to wake, and she wished she could plunge into them, go on dreaming. Forever. She curled up her legs and tightened her arms against her. She knew she didn't want to wake up.

In the next second she jerked full length, eyes staring, wakened with her most basic fear: where were the children? what day was it? what time was it? why was she asleep?

Sunday morning. No school, but church meetings soon. And Richard. Still gone. She heard herself start to groan.

Stiffly, she stretched her legs and arms without lifting her head. Her back ached. She wanted to go back to sleep and wake up and find Richard there beside her. She ran her hands along her arms, down her body. The warmth of her garments under her nightgown comforted her. They called them the garments of the priesthood. It was almost like sleeping in Richard's embrace.

Not the same, though. She had loved that security most about marriage, about being in bed with Richard. She loved being close, breathing together, feeling his arms and legs around her, his voice tingling in her ear. She never tired of that closeness — not always available but often enough to warm and comfort.

When she had told the children to have faith that they'd all be together again and stay that way for eternity, Heather had tugged at her fingers. "When will eternity start?" she'd asked.

Two days ago, Megan nearly answered, but stopped. She was teaching them faith and must not spoil it with her own corrupting fears.

Tears rose against her eyelids. Today she would have to write to her parents, who were on a church mission in Philadelphia. And she would have to call Richard's mother, although she knew the police already had. Probably she wouldn't ask her mother-in-law what she'd meant by telling the police sergeant that Richard never would stay around for a fight. It was an odd thing to say.

"What fight?" Megan had asked the police.

"That's what your mother-in-law said, Mrs. Stevens. Does that mean anything to you?"

"No. I mean . . . a fight with whom? Richard doesn't have any enemies."

"You weren't having any marital problems?"

"No. I told you. Everything was fine. We've never fought. We hardly quarrel, even." Cautiously, she opened her eyes. The Sunday morning flooded her windows with light as golden as the Sundays she remembered from her childhood. Today made a week since she had seen Richard. She felt aching cords pull taut between her joints. She lay as tangled as a snarled marionette.

She closed her eyes again. She could see herself as a little girl on Sunday morning. The dark-haired child skipped between her parents, her dotted-swiss dress swinging as she hopped over the cracks. Megan's dress was the color mother called watermelon. Megan had pretended the flocked white dots were magical seeds. Her sister Paula's dress was sky blue to match her eyes.

This morning, she thought, she must take the children to church. Then she would sit down and write Dear Mama and Papa: I have waited too long to write to you our sad, mysterious news . . . Her cheekbones ached, as she thought of the letter that had been forming in her mind since yesterday.

Suddenly she wished she'd be writing to Paula. She longed for Paula's storm of questions that would be laced with sympathy and outrage. No one ever replaced a sister.

Paula had died years ago in Switzerland in a train accident
during her junior year abroad.

Poor Mama and Papa, Megan thought. First Paula,
now me. Ruined. In what way she was ruined she couldn't
say, but that was the word that came to mind. She was not a
widow, not a divorcee. She had no right to grief or anger or
comfort. Or alimony or insurance benefits. She was nothing. Nowhere.

She sat up, the ache in her neck rising into the bottom of her skull, then higher like milk rising in a baby bottle set on end.

Footsteps thudded in the hall and her bedroom door
swung open.

"I didn't mean to, I didn't mean to, I didn't mean
to," Heather was shrieking and threw herself on the bed.

Megan sighed and ruffled her daughter's hair. "Didn't
mean to what?"

Now Scott, his face white and drawn, trembled beside
the bed. "She broke it!" he managed.

Megan followed the children into the kitchen. The
blue pottery plate Scott had made in Cub Scouts lay on the
floor. Heather stopped crying as they stooped to examine
the plate. "How did this happen?" Megan asked, buying
time.

"She hit it with a ball." Scott's voice dripped dis-
gust, but tears trembled on the edge.

The plate was hopeless, held together only by the
glaze Scott had lavishly applied.

"I only tossed the ball a little way up, Mommy. I
didn't throw it hard."

"I know you didn't mean to." Megan took Heather's hand to pull herself to her feet. "But it was such a beautiful plate." Megan got a piece of cardboard from the desk and slid it gently under the plate. But when she lifted it, the cardboard buckled and the plate disintegrated.

"Oh, give up," Scott said roughly. He took the cardboard and dumped the whole thing into the wastebasket. "I'm late as it is."

She heard the bathroom door shut and the shower turn on. Megan and the girls still used the bathrooms last on Sunday mornings, even though priesthood meeting began at the same time as their Relief Society and Primary meetings. Habit to think men needed to get ready first.

Megan couldn't decide through her headache whether to drive the children to church or walk with them. Elinor settled it. "It's such a pleasant day. We can walk." She spoke with such confidence that the others followed her down the steps.

"Wait," Megan started to say but simply locked the door behind her.

Following them, she wondered if her raw nerves made her perceive everything as luminous. The children's hair shone in the spring sunlight. Their straight, clean legs swung in unison. Scott's shoes showed below his trouser cuffs even though they'd bought his suit for Christmas. Just that detail showed the future—what a fine boy he'd be, and taller than Richard. Strange that she felt her nerves all outside her skin.

When a cab turned the corner she knew Richard was inside. Her mouth went dry and told her so. She watched

it approach, struck by gladness that he would see them at
their most valiant. How nice that he wasn't in a police car
or an ambulance. She turned toward the cab as it neared,
then all the way around, disbelieving, when it passed. She
caught a glimpse of frizzy, white curls in the back seat. Her
knees shook.

"Mom? Mother?" Becky was pulling her arm. The
warm, slightly musty air inside the meeting house drenched
Megan like a soothing bath. The familiar murmurs of neighbors eased her way to the coat hooks. If I'm a pottery plate,
she thought, here is the glaze to seal my cracks.

She thought the air stirred when they walked into
the chapel, then closed around them. She extended her legs
underneath the bench in front of her, deliberately unclenched
her fists and tried to relax her aching shoulders. Her eyes
itched. She dusted the spotless lap of her white linen suit
with a trembling hand.

Soon Nancy lifted her baton and singing rose. Megan
held the hymn book, hearing Becky's soprano on one side of
her and Elinor's wandering monotone on the other.

Lloyd Patterson, Richard's home teaching compan-
ion, prayed in his serious voice that deepened suddenly. "May
thy peace be with the Stevens family," he intoned as Megan's
breath vanished. "May they soon be reunited one with
another. May we, as a ward, be sensitive to their needs."

He went on to the premature Blackham baby. Megan
tried to relax. There'd been no implication that Richard
was dead, yet no hint that he'd deserted them. And that's
not easy, Megan thought, adding her amen to the others.

Scott looked like all the other deacons carrying the

sacrament trays up and down the rows. Only his tight mouth and the short, deep line between his brows gave away his tension. Megan wondered what the other boys had said about his father.

When she took a piece of sacrament bread, she began her weekly audit of her soul but soon stopped. This week her possible inadequacies, her unthinking sins, loomed before her like monsters. She couldn't imagine them. The Lord would have to understand that being in church was all she could do.

When Megan walked into the Relief Society room later, the chatter paused, then began again in an altered tone. Megan flushed and looked for an empty seat. To her surprise, Kristin Johnson, a young divorced mother she hardly knew, smiled warmly and picked up her purse from the chair next to her.

But Megan rushed toward Nancy at the front of the room. She sat down and snatched Benjy from the floor, as if he were her own. Nancy's chuckle assured her that she still belonged. She and Richard, despite everything, must still be cradled within the secure world they had covenanted to endure forever.

4

KRISTIN

You probably think I should take Megan Stevens a casserole," Kristin said to PC, who eyed her narrowly from his favorite footstool. "Well, it's not what she needs. I think I'll take her the phone number for food stamps — and offer her my attorney."

PC yawned. "Oh, but you forget," Kristin added, hands to the floor, her head thrown back on a level with PC, "my attorney's a woman. Otherwise I wouldn't offer. The last thing Megan needs is another male to mess her up, present company excluded from the insult, of course."

Kristin had mentally changed PC's name from Peaches and Cream, his show title, to Prince Charming. The huge Maine Coon neutered male hadn't noticed. Neither had Kristin's daughters.

Kristin dropped to the floor and stretched her heels out straight. Bonny and Sheri were in bed. As usual, Kristin had donned her violet leotard and began her exercises, working out the day's tensions. "You know, about now," she muttered, her nose bouncing gently against her straightened knees, "about bedtime, I mean, Megan is probably pining for a man . . . meaning Richard, of course."

She stood and did a plie grande beside the footstool and stroked the cat, all three feet of him from nose to tail tip. He'd survived the lean years after the divorce only because he ate anything, even the girls' leftover peanut butter sandwiches. "It's a tragedy, PC. All of you and every inch of me slowly growing old."

Kristin still pictured him sprawled on the stone hearth in the house she'd had to sell six months ago. His red-marbled fur had matched the hearth. She imagined he still saw himself that way, too.

At least she'd given PC a good neighborhood, she mused. The neighborhood had been important to her, just hired with her brand new master's degree in pediatric nursing (to go with her brand new divorce). She wanted to move somewhere that didn't mean a great loss of status, even though she and her kids had, of course, dropped on the economic scale, even with child support — when it came.

True, there was only one East Bench. If they had stayed in Salt Lake and just moved from the bench, she wouldn't have been the only divorcee in any city ward. But that was the point, somehow. Even as a novelty, Bountiful told her she still was part of the cream, that her family was not tainted. Besides, she lived close to the clinic, and with the girls in first and third grades, that helped. Still, she knew status mattered to her. She never lied about her own heart.

"Good old PC," she crooned, ruffling his long fur backwards. He blinked in satisfaction. "You know that custody of the cat was the big issue in the divorce? Bryce hated to let me have you, but he knew he'd never win the girls. Not in Utah."

She scooted back from the footstool and began situps while PC lazily licked a huge paw and dabbed between his blue eyes. "You're getting fat," Kristin grunted as she pulled herself up to a sitting position and met his gaze. "Not me, though. I'm getting leaner and meaner by the day." As she clenched her abdominal muscles, she admired the precision her body was achieving and thought about Megan. Megan would probably gain weight, although she found it hard to imagine. Kristin had, as did almost everyone in that situation. You have to do something to fill the hollow inside, Kristin thought.

She'd heard about Richard's disappearance a few days after it happened. Running into Nancy at the grocery store, Kristin got the whole story between the row of cake mixes and the row of pasta: Richard Stevens had disappeared and was believed abducted. Maybe murdered.

At church Sunday morning, she heard the first buzzes hinting at suicide. A Brigham City man had been found dead in a motel two years ago, Julie Taylor was telling people, and no one had ever suspected he had any unusual problems.

She'd watched Megan that Sunday. She couldn't help it. Everyone else was watching her, too. Kristin believed she watched more sympathetically, even if her concern was tainted with a little guilty satisfaction. Right away she'd spotted the golden circle of married women in this ward. Megan, Julie, Nancy, Lisa Thompson, Shannon Winder. The perfect ones, Kristin called them, with both understanding and resentment. She had been perfect once, too, so she knew how vulnerable that status could be. Once you lost your perfection, you never truly felt at home.

Five more situps, she decided, then that's it. She knew what Megan must be getting from the ward. Sympathy, of course, yet estrangement, as well. Then there was her kids' trauma, and on top of that, gut-wrenching worry. At least Kristin would never have to worry about Bryce's welfare. Bryce was just fine. In control. Now. Always. Except for the one way in which he was terribly, horribly wrong.

But Richard? Quiet, humorous, easy-to-talk-to, little-to-say Richard? Kristin stood and stretched again. Richard was nice, exactly the kind of guy she liked without being attracted to. Not enough . . . what? Drive, maybe, although he did well at everything. Not enough spark?

She had this absurd impulse to call Megan, even though they were just church friends. Yet last week in Relief Society, Kristin had watched Megan walk almost blindly into the room and had felt so close to her that she instinctively moved her purse so Megan could sit down. As if Megan would somehow gravitate to her, sensing their bond.

Naturally Megan had been surprised, maybe even offended. Now Kristin smiled ironically and dropped a kiss on PC's snoozing head. She could understand that, she thought, whirling tiptoe across the room, ending with an approximate arabesque. Just as she understood her own guilty contentment at seeing Megan Stevens suddenly made human, single, vulnerable. "Just another sucker like me, BOOM!" Kristin sang to PC, ending with a high kick above his head that shocked his eyes open.

"Come on, PC, it's time to turn in." PC blinked, then looked away. "Come on," she coaxed and snapped her fingers. PC looked at her but didn't budge. Finally she had to lift him from the footstool. He felt heavier than Sheri, who was almost seven.

Moaning a little, he followed her as she snapped off lights, turned down the thermostat and peeked into the girls' room. Small-boned Bonny was sprawled spread-eagle and sound asleep. Sheri had both chubby arms wound around her teddy bear in an embrace that looked too tight for sleep, but she was snoring lightly into the fluffy fur at his neck.

Kristin smiled, then froze. Something in Sheri's pose brought her back to the grocery store where she'd heard of Richard's disappearance, but she didn't remember Nancy, rather Richard himself. She'd passed him there not long ago as she sped along with her basket.

"Hey, *Rich*-ard," she'd sung out, readying her smile for his, prepared to laugh at the wry comment that always seemed at his lips. But he hadn't replied. Hadn't even looked up.

She sat down now on the edge of the bed, stared at Sheri, and tried to remember. What if this was important? Richard had been near the end of one aisle, she remembered, and their little girl — Heather? — was standing in the basket. Her arms were around his neck as if he were lifting her in or out. Kristin knew that stage when kids want to ride but are too big to fit comfortably.

Richard had had his arms around Heather, too, Kristin recalled, crushing her to him, his face buried in the side of her neck. She remembered clearly the worry that thunked in the pit of her stomach. "Did she fall?" she'd asked, regretting her carefree greeting. But by then she really was passing them, puzzled, and Heather twinkled up at her without moving her head.

Heather was all right, she had realized then. But Richard had never looked up, never spoken. Finally Kristin had turned her basket toward the next aisle, her eyebrows raised. It wasn't so much that Richard wasn't aware Kristin had witnessed an emotional moment. No. More as if he hadn't even been there at all.

Now when did I see him? Kristin wondered, walking down the hall toward bed. Should I tell Megan? Was it last month? Five weeks? Six? She couldn't remember. And what did that incident mean, if anything? That he was despondent and the rumors of suicide probably true? That he intended to take off? That he'd had a premonition of trouble, or that he was endangering his family? That he had a incurable disease? Anything. Nothing.

Now she was wound up, too tired to do anything, but not sleepy. She was sorry the girls were asleep. She'd gladly rock one away from a pursuing nightmare. She was sorry she'd put PC on the porch. By now he was asleep, too. Kristin got into bed, picked up a book, then laid it aside. She closed her eyes but in a minute pictured Richard and Bryce, side by side, striding down the sidewalk in suits.

Why don't you home teach your own homes? a woman on a porch screamed at them.

Kristin sat up and smiled. Richard and Bryce had never met. They might have liked each other, though. Bryce would have taken the lead as he always seemed to do.

Not so long ago she'd spent Sunday evenings watching the clock, waiting for Bryce to finish his meetings and come home. He arrived, usually glowing a bit from the spirit of the meeting. The glow turned to heat if she waited in bed.

She could remember what was going on in their lives when Bryce's ardor changed. She'd begun graduate school, and the girls were starting school and pre-school. Small people, not babies any longer. But had Kristin's happiness with her challenge at the university changed her relationship with Bryce? Or was it something quite apart from her? When had she first felt that subtle aversion she didn't understand? She didn't know — only that it began her worst nightmare.

With her eyes closed she could still see him come through the bedroom doors. Not in her present tiny bedroom but through the double doors in the house on the east bench of Salt Lake. She saw the shine of his copper hair, the gleam in his eyes, the straight set of his shoulders under his suit coat.

He'd been one of the perfect ones. He always looked perfect, at least. He was what she'd wanted, still wanted. So gradually, she could never trace it, he'd stopped wanting her. That still hurt. About the same time he became superdad, teasing, demanding, cajoling, rough-housing, tickling, snuggling with their daughters.

Now she chilled thinking about that change. But then she'd shoved her pangs of jealousy aside and bragged about him as a wonderful father. She'd admired his devotion to the role of fatherhood, even though his ardor in the bedroom was less. Maybe that just showed his maturity, his spiritual growth. She didn't know. No one talked about things like that.

Bonny was only six, about Sheri's age now, when Bryce started tucking the girls in late at night. Kristin thought the ritual sweet, and it gave her a few minutes to study. Then for months, as his ritual took longer and longer, she stopped thinking about it entirely. Almost. At least, she tried not to think about it. But one night, with a sense of dread that astonished her, she forced her trembling legs down the hall and saw him leaning over their daughters as they slept or seemed to sleep. She could see only Bonny's bare legs past Bryce's back, her underpants around one ankle. She heard Bonny whimper. She had never known for sure whether Bonny was asleep or awake.

Then the nightmare began for Kristin in earnest. More nightmare than she could bear to recall even now. She never should have coped for so long, except she'd had such hope that everything could be worked out. At last she'd packed their suitcases one Sunday evening and called a cab before Bryce came home. Monday morning she'd signed a complaint against him, then cried herself sick in the attorney's office. That night both Bryce and the bishop had called her cold as she faced them dry-eyed.

Kristin pointed her toes and stretched her body, her arms full length, slowly turning her head from side to side.

All her muscles were tensed. She couldn't imagine how Megan would deal with Bryce, but she'd not been able to imagine herself dealing with him either. Yet she had. And Megan could cope, too. That was the secret she had to share, even if Megan didn't want to hear it. Yet.

Still, they were bound to become friends. The ward would see to that. Only today Nancy had told Kristin the visiting teaching assignments had been adjusted. She and Megan would be partners. Kristin had pretended not to hear Nancy drop this on Megan with a blithe, "We thought you two would be good for each other." She could do without Megan's hurt eyes, her forced smile.

After several tries, she and Megan set aside an evening to visit the three women assigned to them. Kristin walked over to Megan's house, savoring the almost-evening air, the delicate turquoise of the sky. Clumps of buds on the trees' smallest twigs were outlined against the fading light.

"Hi," she said casually when Megan closed the door behind her without asking Kristin in. "How are you doing?"

"Just fine," Megan said with a face so taut it took Kristin aback. They walked for nearly a block without saying anything. Kristin searched for a way to ease Megan's tension, to let her that it was all right, to relax. But to know that Kristin, a divorced woman, understood, would only make her feel worse. Kristin kept quiet.

Megan broke the silence when they came to Sister Harris's walk. She stopped and stood absolutely still.

Kristin waited. Megan looked at her, and Kristin was shocked by the flatness in her eyes, as if no one lived behind them. Then Megan's lip twitched and her face rearranged itself. "I can't do it. I'm sorry, Kristin. I can't go in there."

"Let's do Sister Harris on our way back." Kristin wondered why talkative, concerned, over-sixty Sister Harris was so frightening.

"No, that won't help. It's just that . . . ," she sighed. Her eyes appealed for understanding. "I just can't answer any more questions. I mean, I know people are concerned, and I'd tell them the answers if I knew them. But . . . ," her voice trailed.

"Right," Kristin said so that Megan could stop talking in that frayed tone. Kristin's relief that she was not the one who was upsetting Megan let her relax and take charge.

"Don't worry," Kristin said. "I know a few defense tactics. If those fail, we'll just both stare her down." She put on a fierce face, and Megan smiled. By the time they walked up the steps, they were picturing that glare turned on sweet Sister Harris, who found them giggling when she opened the door.

The visits became a game. Kristin launched into their prescribed message on charity before the conversation could lag or wander. Megan punched in stories and examples that cast her in a positive, not a pitiful, light. When any of their sisters leaned forward sympathetically, Kristin unleased a staccato of questions. How were Sister Smith's grandchildren? Where had Sister Marelli bought her figurines? Was Sister Harris's aged mother still going to come to stay with her? Once those were answered, a glance toward Megan was sufficient for both to hoist their purse straps to their shoulders, and they were gone in a cloud of good cheer.

"Hey, you're good at this!" Megan said, laughing with relief as they walked home. "You don't know how much I appreciate it."

Kristin winced. Megan's tone cast herself as the tragic heroine. The only tragic heroine.

"Yes. I do." Maybe someday Kristin would tell her.

There was a silence. Megan was watching her, she could feel along the side of her face. "Yes. I guess you must," Megan said.

Kristin waited. Now would come the hint that a divorce, probably from some slob, was not comparable to the disappearance of a loved husband. It wasn't, of course, but Megan didn't know the whole story. No one here did. Kristin glanced to the side, but Megan wasn't there.

Megan had frozen in her tracks again. Kristin took a few steps back. "What is it?"

Megan's face was stricken, guilty even, but she shook her head a little, smiled crookedly, and caught up with short, jerky steps. "Really," she said then, trying for the normality she'd found for their ladies, "one has no idea how people feel until something happens. I mean . . ."

She gave up.

Kristin took a deep breath. "Yes, but after that, you understand everything." She shrugged.

Megan nodded and there was another pause. "Kris," she said then, "I'm sorry. I never realized . . ."

Now Kristin stopped. Megan's eyes were full. Kristin had expected this recognition, had hoped for it, months from now. Maybe years. Not when Megan was still in such pain. She felt her throat close. In a second they'd be weeping in each other's arms, right in front of Nancy's house, too. Wouldn't the ward love that one?

"You're going through hell, Megan. I'd have called or come over, but I just didn't think you'd . . . "

They walked up Megan's front walk. "Can you come in for a while?"

Kristin checked her watch. "I'd love to, but I promised the girls I'd quiz them for their spelling test tomorrow. How about a rain check?"

"Okay. Soon though."

"Right. Oh, Meg? Someone told me you're pregnant?"

"I am. Four months now."

"But you look thin, thinner than before."

Megan smiled. "Don't worry. I'll turn mammoth soon enough. I've lost a few pounds from the stress. I've just had too much on my mind to give this pregnancy much thought."

"When do you see the doctor next?"

"A week from Friday. Why? Do you think there's a problem?" Now Megan looked worried. "He's been at a convention, so I made the appointment for when he'd be back."

The nurse in Kristin was definitely concerned, but she smiled. "Hope not. But why don't you call me after your appointment and tell me everything's all right."

"Okay. Thanks." Megan seemed satisfied.

Kristin walked home slowly. The sky had faded to gray and the budded trees looked knobby. A chilly breeze from the canyon wound around her neck, her legs. She'd been right. She and Megan would become friends. But at what cost? A weariness as old and as walked-on as the dust that brushed over her mouth weighted her body. Tonight she and PC would go to bed early and dream of running and pouncing.

5

SCOTT

Scott tried to imagine his own eyes open in the dark.
    His eyes were light blue, like his father's. Would they
be visible to someone coming through the open bedroom
door? Would they gleam like a cat's? If Dad came home and
peeked into his room (probably first thing), would he see
Scott's open eyes even before Scott made out his father's
form in the dark?

    Sometimes Scott thought he saw his father standing
in the doorway, hands at the top of his back pockets, one
shoulder a little lower than the other, his head tipped in that
listening way. Even if he never saw his face, Scott would
know him anywhere—just by that posture. Even if his face
had been disfigured in an accident, Scott would know him.

    And most likely he *would* see his father first when he
came home. In fact, one especially lonely night Scott had
promised himself that like a blood vow. He had plenty of

time to make vows, time to think things through. Now that Dad was gone, Scott's body had forgotten how to sleep. Nights, he lay in his dark room, his heart racing like it did before a midnight hike. When morning came, he felt he'd only blinked, if that. He kept track of the hours on his digital alarm clock. Sometimes he played his radio on twenty-four hour news stations. Often he fell asleep at school.

A couple of nights after Dad disappeared, Becky had come into Scott's room and sat down on the end of his bed. If he'd been asleep he would have been startled, but he saw the soft outline of her flowing hair and robe as she rustled through the door.

"We're the oldest. We have to talk," she'd said.

He sat up and turned back the covers uncertainly, but she grabbed the top quilt and pulled it to the end of the bed, covering her bent knees. Of course they were too old now to snuggle under the covers as they used to. Suddenly he was embarrassed at his gesture. "Okay," he said. His voice sounded hoarse.

There was a silence. He was afraid Becky might cry, so he asked tentatively, "What do you think?"

"An accident, I guess. And if it's an accident we'll hear about it pretty soon, won't we?"

Scott thought it over. "I think we'd already have heard about it by now. He was just on the bus."

"Yes, but he might have gone somewhere in a car with someone. You know, a friend or someone at work. They might have gotten into an accident."

"But Bec, his boss would have known. Or the police. That person would be missing, too."

Becky sighed. "Then it has to be foul play. What else? Mom and Dad have never fought or anything. If they were having trouble, don't you think we'd know about it?"

Scott thought about that until Becky shifted her weight and sighed in exasperation. "They wouldn't tell us," he said finally. "I can't see them telling us they can't get along."

"But we'd know if things were so bad Dad would leave. And Mom's pregnant, Scott. Dad would never leave her when she's pregnant. That'd be tacky."

A pause. Scott felt offended, as if Becky had said Dad was tacky, which he wasn't. What she was saying was that he wasn't tacky, but still . . . "Maybe he didn't want her to be pregnant," he suggested.

Becky gasped. "How do you think she got that way? You mean you think it's our fault? That he's tired of all of us kids?"

"Not us. Hey, Bec, please don't cry. I mean, you know, maybe he didn't want an additional baby."

He said a word under his breath so Becky wouldn't hear. No point in making things worse. Becky was sobbing her confession into the quilt. "I keep thinking that if I'd just been nicer, if I hadn't gotten mad that day when he grounded me for toilet papering Polly's house . . . "

Scott's mouth and throat felt packed with cotton. He'd heard somewhere that was what they did with corpses. He reached for the glass of water he kept on his nightstand. "Come on, Bec, you know it's not that."

To his relief, she wiped off her face on a corner of the quilt and breathed deeply through her mouth. "I know.

I mean, it's normal for kids to do stuff like that, but it's not normal for father to just vanish."

Now she sounded furious. Scott sighed. He wished she would go away and leave him to his thoughts. He lay back and listened to her talk out theories. None of them made much sense, but speculating out loud helped her.

Finally she shook out her curls and said, "Well, I guess I'd better get a little sleep. Don't worry, Scott. It'll be all right."

"Good night."

He watched her leave. Becky never could forget she was a year older than he. One minute they were friends, the next she mothered him like that. Sometimes he thought Mom treated Dad that way, too.

He didn't worry, as Becky evidently did, that Dad's disappearance was his fault. When Scott had realized his father was absent, a memory as clear as seeing a movie a second time had come to him. Since he was at the kitchen table eating cornflakes for breakfast when he heard about Dad disappearing, the smell of cornflakes was now inextricably mixed with the memory of snow camping with Dad and the scouts in January.

The first night of the camp he and Dad had walked a little way to look at the stars, which dappled the sky like frosty snow. Scott and Dad stood in silence under a giant fir for a long time. then, as Scott began to shiver, Dad had put an arm around him and pulled him close. "Scotter, I want you to remember one thing as long as you live, no matter what happens."

Scott waited, perhaps a minute or two. He thought

maybe his father was going to say something about God or the church or Joseph Smith. What he said surprised Scott, but it fit. It fit still.

"Nothing, Scott, can separate a man and his son. They are joined by blood, genes, priesthood. Every cell in me is in you. Do you understand?"

Scott nodded, or tried to within that hard embrace. His father held him like that until his shoulders ached. Then they walked quietly back to their tent. Later Scott's body jerked him awake in his down sleeping bag. He looked around wildly in the dark, feeling he had overlooked something important. "It's all right, son," Dad said then, "go back to sleep."

The next day, Scott had looked up from the campfire at his father's drawn face and realized that the comforting voice in the night had been alert, not clouded with sleep.

Now ashy smudges had formed under Scott's eyes. He looked like Dad the second day of the camp, or when all the researchers had to work overtime right before the legislature met.

He was like his Dad. He knew that being a son was important. He had known since he was very small that his father loved Bec, and later Elinor and Heather. But in some ways it was Scott who really counted. He could tell it by the way Dad said, "Bring it here, son." Or, "Give me a hand, son." Son and Scott were both his names. One fit the other like an innertube inside a tire.

Now Scott listened, but the house was quiet, his sisters in bed. He got up and silently walked down the carpeted hall. His parents' bedroom door was open, but the room was dark. He decided that no one was in there, so he stepped inside and turned on the reading lamp by the bed.

He didn't like to go in this room now. He wondered if Dad had disliked those fluffy white curtains or the heavy white spread on the bed. Maybe Dad had wanted a fur spread — a tiger skin like the one advertised on a waterbed in the catalog. Maybe Dad had even wanted a waterbed. Maybe Mom had refused. But, Scott had to admit guiltily, Mom didn't refuse anybody much of anything.

There had to be some reason. Since Scott didn't know what, he assumed the answer was in this orderly space his parents could close the door on, leaving him and his sisters and their hassles outside, looking at their own faces on the mirrored half of the double doors.

Somewhere in here were Dad's sterling silver cuff-links. They were engraved RSS. Dad's initials, and Scott's, too. If he could find them, Scott decided, he would take them and keep them until Dad came back. It seemed right. He couldn't see them anywhere, though, and his hands hung heavy when he considered going through drawers. The cuff-links, just the image of them, seemed to bring Dad closer.

"What was it, Dad?" he whispered.

He pulled the mirrored door into the room and stood opposite it, his hands at the tops of his back pockets. He shifted his weight a little to one side, dropping one shoulder. His bones were growing long and angular. Dark-ringed eyes looked back at him. He tilted his head. Like Dad, he would be quite good looking in a reasonable way.

Suddenly, a strangled gasp made him leap, heart knocking, away from the mirror. He wheeled and found himself clutching his mother by both arms. He felt her nails dig into his biceps for a second. Her eyes, almost on a level with his, were wide with shock and hope. They held each other, trembling, then came apart, angry and apologetic all at once.

"Were you looking for me?" Mom said, "or . . . "

"Uh, no, just . . . well, I wondered about those cuf-flinks. Dad's cufflinks."

"Which cufflinks, Scott?"

"You know. The ones you gave him with his initials on."

"Oh." She sat down on the edge of the bed, reached up and pulled him down beside her. She looked at him a long time, her eyes seeming to read a story in his face. For some reason he recalled the way her hand used to brush over his cheeks and brow when he was sick. He felt sorry for her and looked away.

"Scott," she asked finally, "do you want those cufflinks?"

"Just until Dad comes back. I thought I'd keep them for him until then."

"I see." She was quiet for a minute, then sighed. "Scott, I think I'd rather keep them in here. I know they're your initials, too. If Dad doesn't come back, the cufflinks are yours."

Scott opened his mouth to protest.

"I know," she said hurriedly, "I think he will, too. But if he doesn't, the cufflinks are yours when you turn eighteen." She leaned forward and kissed him lightly on the forehead. "That isn't so long, is it?"

"Five years," Scott said, standing up.

Scott went back to his room and cried in the dark. He felt like a knight who'd gone after a treasure or something else of great value — a name? — only to be patted on the head and sent back home to grow up. He burrowed under the blankets so no one would hear his shameful cries: I want my dad! I want my dad!

MEGAN

Megan sat in the car after meetings on Sunday, waiting for Becky to come out of the red brick chapel. They were all going to dinner at the stake Relief Society president's house. Megan felt uncomfortable about it, and the kids were almost sullen. They really didn't know Gail Skinner, but she had insisted and Megan hadn't had the energy to resist.

Scott was staring in stubborn silence out the windshield, opposite her in the front seat. He always rode in the front seat now, unless one of the girls beat him to it. Becky, particularly, resented his determination. She was the oldest. Elinor and Heather were arguing about something in back, but Megan let their voices tumble past her; they were no more than chipmunks chattering in the canyon.

Turning the calendar to May had hit Megan like a physical blow. April hadn't been so bad — Richard had vanished only weeks ago. But May — more than a month — made his absence as awful and imperative as vomit on the floor. She watched family after family come out of the church. She scanned their faces, smiling, dissatisfied, tense, tired, or expectant. Somewhere there must be a clue to the secret they held so lightly; the one that had escaped her. None of them look happier than we did, she thought.

Maybe they had been too content, too peaceful? Maybe they hadn't let out their anger often enough? Maybe frustrations had built up. She didn't think so, though. Elinor and Heather were about ready to come to blows now. Was that so different than a few months ago? Maybe a little. All their nerves were frayed.

"Stop it, now," she said, ignoring their protests and reasons. She couldn't possibly referee.

The families were thinning now, just stragglers came down the walk: a busy priesthood holder catching up with his wife, three deacons Scott's age, laughing together. Pretty soon Becky would come, too, in the center of her clique. For just a second, Megan seized the idea that Richard would walk down that sidewalk, nonchalant, squinting at the sky to see if it would rain. He would be alone, hands jammed in the pockets of his suit coat, shoes shuffling just slightly in that way he had when he was relaxed.

Gone, Megan thought, realizing that every passing family had diminished her. Gone.

She wondered about calling Sister Skinner and telling her she was sick, they couldn't come. But then she thought of all the trouble she'd gone to preparing dinner. She couldn't do it. As soon as Becky came she would snap to attention.

Would smile and speak to the children. Would start the car. But not quite yet.

———————

That night, sitting up in bed, Megan felt the hollowness return. Nothing she had eaten or said or heard, none of the nervous, congenial laughter, had filled up even an atom of the vacuum.

He's dead, she told herself. He'd been tense, maybe depressed. He took his own life. For the moment, it seemed credible. She had seen him in moods where he looked ashen, strained, unreachable. At such a moment she could imagine him walking off and . . . doing what? Not pulling the trigger of a gun. Not Richard. Driving off a canyon road? Maybe. Sitting under a tree and waiting for a soft, freezing sleep high in the mountains? But he hadn't had a car. Those endings seemed ludicrously impractical. By the time he figured out the logistics, surely he would have reconsidered. Or if he acted too impulsively, he'd have been found.

"Gone," she whispered, trying it out. The word lodged in the darkness. No light showed behind her curtains tonight. It was overcast, promising rain.

She sighed and stretched her legs and arms, which were cramped with tension. She rolled back her head and turned it in a slow circle. If Richard were dead, though, that meant, in a way, he was still with them. Wouldn't his spirit seek atonement? Wouldn't he stay close to them?

She had heard widows bear testimony to that clear, warm presence that came to them from time to time, that lingered as they raised their children. She believed them.

She folded her arms across her body and felt the

reassuring cling of her garments along her skin. She missed him, purely and deeply. She closed her eyes and imagined him tipped back in bed against the pillows. He'd be talking about something. What someone said in priesthood meeting. Anything. Maybe they'd talked small talk all those years: what the kids said, what was going on in the ward or at work, where to go on vacation. It had been so easy, so pleasant, so comfortable. She could hear the exact tenor of his voice, its ironic edge, the dry chuckle.

Maybe he'd reach for her and kiss her neck the way he did when he wanted her. He usually left her alone when she was pregnant, but she didn't show much. Her eyes burned behind their lids.

Richard? she started to whisper, but her throat would barely let the word escape. She waited. The emptiness grew so great, minute by minute, that it seemed like one of the black holes in space Scott talked about. Any second it would suck her in, devour the remains of her world.

Megan noticed that she was no longer looking into the dark but staring at the telephone near her bed. What was she expecting? A call from the next world?

Grimly amused, she found she could not move her eyes from it. Perhaps it held some kind of clue. Trembling, she reached out, picked up the cool, plastic receiver, and held it against her ear. It felt hard, solid, smooth. In her ear, the dial tone sang until a recorded voice told her to hang up.

In the next instant, she bounded out of bed and ran for the bathroom. She vomited, retching again and again, until she was empty. For the next few days, she vomited frequently. Morning sickness, she told herself, but this wan't like the morning sickness she had had before. Now it was as if her body was determined to become as hollow as her home — as if, having failed to hold Richard, she could hold nothing at all. Friday morning a dream woke her. As she stared at the two peaks her knees made under the blanket, the dream became a memory of Richard on the Monday morning he disappeared. Richard was saying, "Heather's croup sounds better."

Megan had only murmured, "Mmmm," exhausted from steaming Heather at 3 a.m. Besides, thick, acid-laced nausea rolled in her stomach.

Richard's tone, clearly remembered now, shocked Megan upright in bed. Why had he checked Heather at all? He wasn't usually worried enough to do that, especially when he must know Megan had been up with her. Was he just worried or . . . ?

Megan jumped out of bed and headed for the bath-tub. Even in the warm water the memory surrounded her like mist. For so long she'd been unable to remember that morning. What did it mean to wake with that fragment lying in her mind like a knife? A simple comment hanging in the air, a perfectly usual goodby. A peck meant for her cheek that caught one half-awake ear.

"For heaven's sake," Megan said aloud when she picked up the garments she'd dropped on the hamper. There was blood again, this time more than the usual few drops. She remembered Kristin's concern. Her heart tightened.

But she knew about miscarriage. She'd waited one out with Wendy, her friend in her former ward. She'd seen the stream of blood that became a flood at the end. This patch (that's all it was, really, she told herself) was just a symptom of stress. Still, she should mention it to the doctor.

Megan was not surprised when the children were disorganized and quarrelsome, late getting off to school. Obviously, it was that kind of morning, and summer vacation was close now. It seemed predictable that the doorbell would ring just as she put her car keys into her purse and picked up her checkbook.

"Scoot over to Nancy's," she told Heather as she opened the door. "I'll see you later." Nancy was still willing to tend, but now she never asked Megan to return the favor.

"Mrs. Stevens?" She looked up from Heather's departing figure to see a man in a gray cotton suit.

"Yes."

"Mrs. Richard Stevens?"

"Yes. Why do you ask?" Fear jolted down her spine into her legs. He didn't look like a police officer, not quite. He introduced himself and she nodded, then promptly forgot his name.

"You are aware that your husband took out a personal loan several months ago?"

"What? No, he didn't. We didn't get a loan."

He showed her a contract with Richard's familiar signature at the bottom.

Megan looked at the large loop in the R until she felt dizzy. "Really," she wanted desperately to be able to say, "I can't talk to you now. I'm pregnant and I have to go to the doctor. It took me five minutes to find my car keys and I've been feeling awful, and . . . " Thinking that, she realized how she ached everywhere, had ached for weeks.

"May I come in, Mrs. Stevens?"

She stood aside and he walked past her. He sat down on the couch. He showed her the contract again, and she took it. She read it over and over, trying to make sense through a blur of growing panic.

"The loan was issued on March 18, Mrs. Stevens."

Megan's vision went black, except for a round hole at the center, which she focused on the man's face. "When did he get the money?"

"Let's see. He was given cash—he specified that— on Monday, March 21."

"I see." But what? She felt Richard's mouth against her ear.

"So, Mrs. Stevens, there is an outstanding debt to our company of $2,500. No payments have been made."

"He's gone," Megan told him.

"I beg your pardon?"

"He's missing. He disappeared. The police have been looking for him, but they haven't found him."

"You haven't heard from him."

"Not a word." Suddenly she was so angry she thought she would erupt in a shower of sparks. She pressed her lips together and stared down at her folded hands. A large, freck-led hand suddenly covered hers. She jumped.

"Mrs. Stevens, please. I didn't know. I'm sorry."

Megan looked at him, surprised. "I'm all right."

"Just a few more questions, if you don't mind. I really

am sorry." His face did look sorry, professionally sorry, like a mortician's. Megan tried for the same moderation.

"When did your husband leave?"

"That day."

"That day being . . . "

"March 21."

"And you haven't heard from him since?"

"No."

He looked at her for a long minute, then shuffled his papers again. "This may not help you very much, Mrs. Stevens, but your husband did insure this loan."

"What does that mean?"

"It means that for an additional hundred dollars the loan was insured so that if something happened to him you wouldn't have to repay the money."

"Really?" she swallowed. "But the police haven't found a body. Our life insurance won't pay. The state doesn't want to help us. Even your company might think this proves . . . " She caught herself.

"It doesn't prove anything, Mrs. Stevens. Now I know there are some who would say it does, but your husband might have borrowed that money for a good reason, maybe to surprise you with . . . a piano or something. Why, carrying that cash around might be the reason something happened to him."

He stood and walked to the door, smiling back his sorry smile. "We just don't know, do we?"

After he left, Megan sat down abruptly, then dialed the clinic and asked for Kristin. She waited while the receptionist transferred the call. Her hand rattled the receiver against her jaw.

"Kristin. I'm on my way to the doctor. You know, he's in your building. Is there any chance you could . . . go with me?"

"Is this your regular appointment?" Kristin's voice sounded professional, but Megan found it comforting. "Or are you bleeding or cramping?"

"Both. It is my regular appointment — a little late — and I'm just spotting. But this morning has been strange. I just found out something about Richard."

"What, Megan?"

"He had money. He took out a loan right before he . . . went away."

She heard Kristin's breath, a loud, long gush. "I'll meet you in your doctor's waiting room. Are you sure you can drive over?"

"After today I'll be able to do anything."

"You'd better believe it," Kristin told her.

The car knew its way to the clinic, it had traveled the route so often. Megan felt calm, detached, but interested, as if she were opening the final chapter in a mystery. Remembering that last morning after so many weeks of unbroken uncertainty was an odd comfort. The memory formed a small piece of certitude, something solid if ambiguous.

She stopped at a red light. She couldn't believe that Richard would willfully leave them to all this — the uncertainty, the insecurity, the need to write family and friends, the unanswered questions in the ward, the neighborhood, the grief, and the confusion in their own hearts. Hadn't he

known how Scott would sleepwalk, his hand fluttering before
him? When Megan had grasped his shoulders and said,
"Scott, it's all right," the boy had blurted, eyes still shut,
"Dad!"

Richard wouldn't have stayed in the same room while
she called the bishop and asked for his help. He wouldn't
have gone grocery shopping with the Relief Society president and blinked back tears as she wrote out the check.
Richard, who reviewed restaurant tabs meticulously, then
insisted on paying, would never have survived the humiliation.

Richard would never have sat through the interview
at the state welfare office while Megan tried to figure out
what to do next. One look at the office of tense women
overseeing their playing children would have sent him on;
but then, what social worker would have kept Richard waiting?

He'd always loved Megan's flair for dressing herself
and the children; he liked how she arranged the house. Could
he wish her humbled like this? Did he secretly want her
punished?

Yet he'd done their income tax early, she remembered, and mailed it in. He'd taken out a loan and insured
it so she wouldn't have to pay it back. Had he planned to
pay — or not?

She turned into the parking lot and began looking
for a space. No, she could not believe that Richard would
wish for them these tortures. But she knew how he could
close one door and open another. Wasn't she the one who
sent his mother birthday cards, a Christmas gift, a Mother's

Day plant? When they'd told their Salt Lake friends goodby, Richard had never looked back. Megan had kept in touch with Wendy and the others for nearly a year. It was Richard who could set down his leather-working kit one day and the next bring home a tank and tropical fish afloat in a plastic bag.

She waited while an elderly couple pulled their Volkswagen out of a parking place near the clinic entrance, then swung the car expertly into the slot. Richard would not imagine any of this. And for that, wherever he was, Megan could and did condemn him.

Nothing the doctor said made any sense. Megan knew only that he couldn't find her baby with his probing fingers, couldn't sound it out with his stethoscope. "You're smaller than when you first came in," he said at last. "This is not a pregnant uterus."

"We're sorry you lost it," the nurse said when Megan and Kristin finally left. The nurse's look told Megan she had been careless, that perhaps she should check under the seats in her car. A baby could be lost anywhere, it seemed, if you didn't pay close attention.

"But I didn't lose my baby," she told Kristin, who had somehow left work and was driving her home.

"We call this an AB mis," Kristin said, watching Megan instead of the road. "The body absorbs most of the fetus. Sometimes there's not much bleeding."

Megan thought about it. "I feel almost as if I ate it up."

Kristin touched her hand lightly. "An AB can be awfully traumatic. And the fetus is toxic in your system, too. I think if you're going to miscarry, better to have the whole mess happen and be over with."

When they pulled into the driveway Megan said, "Richard had money."

"Yes, you told me that on the phone. How do you know?"

Megan told her, then told about her memory of that Monday morning. Retelling it, something snagged in her thoughts like a neglected clue.

But Kristin hugged her then. "Come on. Your kids are going to be home soon."

Megan trailed Kristin to the house, marveling at how quickly Kristin found the right key and opened the door. She floated behind her to the bedroom and obeyed when Kristin said to undress and lie down. "But I'm all right," she protested, charmed by her own compliance. "I mean, nothing's different than when I left this morning."

"You've had enough shock to flatten an elephant," Kristin said. The anger in her voice warmed Megan like the quilt Kristin pulled up to her chin. I'm shivering, Megan noticed, but I'm not cold.

Now Kristin was standing beside her with pills and a glass of water. Time seemed to be moving in gulps and pauses. "The doctor sent these home for you."

"What are they?"

"This is a morning-after pill. It'll get your periods going again and you'll feel better sooner. This one is to help you relax."

While Megan hovered peacefully above the bed in a warm cloud, she listened to the house function without her.

Dimly she heard the children come home from school. They didn't bring their day's scrapes and troubles to her. Once she heard other voices and strained through the cloud until she realized the voices belonged to Kristin's daughters. She hunted for their names, then gave up, but she was pleased to think of Kristin caring for all those children.

Not until the night showed outside the curtains, black and dotted with stars, did her children come in carrying a glass of ice water. Megan drank a little and strained to see them clearly.

"We came to say good night," Scott told her.

Becky bent and kissed her forehead. "We're sorry about the baby, Mom."

Scott nodded vigorously.

Megan tried to smile, felt her throat close, and shook her head a little.

"Are you feeling any better?" Scott asked hopefully.

She gulped. "I'll be fine." Scott looked relieved and nodded.

"Kristin says our father went away," Elinor said in her blunt way. "Kristin says it's not your fault and we should help you more."

"Of course it's not her fault," Becky cried, glaring at Elinor. She sweetened her voice. "Now you'd better get some rest, Mom."

"I'm just so groggy," Megan said. "I'll be better tomorrow. Are you doing all right?"

"We're fine, Mommy," Heather chirped, pressing her head against the quilt. The others nodded, smiling at her, haloed in the lamplight, then swirling slightly as Megan felt the cloud brush her cheek. They kissed her one by one; she heard the click of the lamp, then darkness took her in as her eyelids sank.

But even then her mind was clear. Why had Kristin told the children? What had she told them? About the loan? About the miscarriage? Why hadn't she waited to let Megan tell them herself? She sighed. Tomorrow she would straighten things out. Not now.

As Megan's mind circled, the morning's memory returned, and suddenly the snag hooked into sense. "Heather's croup sounds better," Richard had said. Hearing his voice again, she found the relief in it, the profound relief. Yet Heather had had croup before and was no sicker this time. Richard sounded as if Heather's improvement took care of everything.

Considering that, Megan realized that her bed was gory with loss, with a deliberate deprivation that wore no apology. She drew up her knees and let her heavy arms fall across them closing in whatever it was she had left.

Dimly, she heard Kristin's voice chasing the children's voices down the hall toward their rooms. How strange that, falling toward sleep, Megan felt light fill and warm her. Her eyelids prickled with grateful tears. She had only moments to wonder why, after this day of disasters, she felt encompassed and transfused by love.

KRISTIN

L ittle snot," Kristin muttered as Becky swept by her without so much as a glance. The tight cluster of girls in pastel dresses turned down the aisle in the chapel, stringing into a pew near the back.

Becky had been sweet and subdued the day Kristin brought Megan back from the clinic. Poor kids, Kristin had thought. First their dad gone, now their mom in bed, and the baby they'd planned on gone too. She didn't think they had really envisioned the baby, though. They took that news calmly.

After calling her girls and telling them to come over, Kristin had cooked dinner. She debated, watching them all fork down rice and hamburger curry, whether to resolve for them what Megan could not.

She knew Megan. She was like most people in the valley. Whatever could be left unsaid might just as well not exist. Except it did. She could imagine these children going from week to week, month to month, wondering what had become of their father. She couldn't tell them where he was, of course, but they could stop painting him as a fallen hero. It was Megan who had not deserted them, Megan who was miscarrying, Megan who needed their help and sympathy. Kristin knew how children worked. Show a little vulnerability and they go for the jugular. She would spare Megan this, if nothing else.

As they munched her quick-from-scratch brownies, she told them their father had left. Becky wept.

"Where did he go?" wondered Heather.

"I don't know," Kristin answered. "I don't know where he went or why. I wish I did."

"There's got to be a reason," Scott said fiercely. Kristin watched as Becky lifted her head and met his eyes.

"Maybe we should put an ad in the newspaper," Elinor suggested.

Scott scoffed. "Sure. Lost: one father. Reward for safe return."

"Exactly," Elinor said, unintimidated.

"Well, your mother didn't leave you. And she needs your help," Kristin began.

But with that, their attention shifted. The telephone rang. Elinor and Scott argued over whose turn it was to clear the table, and Sheri began to complain that PC would be starving at home. "Oh, shut up!" Becky had screamed at them, wiping tears with the flats of both hands as she ran toward the telephone.

Now, at church, Becky seemed not to have a care.

She was one of the pack of girls that ran things in the ward. Younger and less popular girls gave way before the intimidation of the clique's rather deliberate charm. Becky wouldn't risk her spot in that bunch for anything, Kristin realized. Let alone by talking to a divorcee. Not now.

Kristin found a seat and smiled, remembering her own group — Patty, Micki, Carol, and Gwynn. Gwynn had called the shots when Kristin was sixteen, and Kristin would have died rather than offend.

Bonny and Sheri were on the stand with Elinor and little Heather. She could see Scott's back where he sat with the rest of the deacons along the first row. Funny. Now she kept an eye on six kids instead of two. This was progress?

Next to Scott sat Brad Wesley, the Korean boy Harvey and Lois Symth had adopted ten years ago. Brad and his younger brother Chip, a black child from the Philadelphia slums, both passed the sacrament now. They were the only minority students at the junior high school and a source of pride there and in the ward since both were honor students. Kristin felt a pang every time she saw them, though. She ached for their difference, especially as they approached dating age and would be exotic dolls no longer. She knew what it was like to be the person everyone remembers to love. Tolerance is fine if you like to be tolerated, she thought, then found a smile for Megan, sliding in beside her.

As Megan set down her purse, Kristin wondered whether Becky was wincing at her mother's choice of seats. Status, status, she sighed

"I've done it now," Megan whispered.

"What?"

"I just offered to help Nancy finish sewing for her sister's wedding. Six bridesmaids and three flower girls. Can you believe it?"

"Are you into masochism or something?" Kristin answered. But she could see the happiness in Megan's face. She heard Becky's bunch giggling in the back of the chapel.

The sacrament song brought her back to the meeting, and she kept her thoughts still while the bread and water were passed slowly along each row. The children were in the choir seats to present the annual Primary program. Kristin enjoyed watching the kids' antics, which usually provided a counterpoint to their more solemn message — except when the distraction was provided by Sheri, as it was now, sitting cross-legged in the high-armed chair so that her underpants showed plainly.

"Terrific," Kristin muttered. Megan smiled slightly, as if she were sympathetic but not really noticing.

Already Jimmy Sheldon in the back row of the choir seats was crossing his eyes. Rumor was that he'd done it for years during Primary programs. When he turned twelve next year and became a deacon, he'd be sitting in front where Scott was. Then only the bishopric and speakers could get the effect of those incandescent green eyes examining one another.

Kristin glanced casually around the chapel. Marie Sheldon was staring brightly at the bishop, who was introducing the program. No doubt she would keep her eyes off her son, her only defense against what she could not remotely control.

The program linked freedom in America with the

sanctity of the traditional family: a father, a mother, and children all living happily in tidy cottages. Or something like that. Kristin groaned. The theme would give her a headache, but what about Megan? Already an interested smile was glued to Megan's mouth like a false moustache.

"Does this mean we're not Americans?" Kristin whispered. Megan just glanced at her, puzzled.

Kristin sighed deeply, slid down slightly on the bench and crossed her ankles. Megan had told her not long ago about how she had gathered the children together the first Monday after Richard had left and tried to have family home evening as usual. "It was awful," Megan had afterwards confided, her voice incredulous. "Here I thought I was being so brave, carrying on just as Richard and the church would expect me to. I expected it of myself! But the children stared at me as if I was betraying them somehow, or betraying their father. No one would talk. But the next week we didn't have it, and Scott asked me about it the next morning at breakfast. So much like Richard. He sounded like I'd next be leaving the church."

"You can't win," Kristin sympathized. "So play games on Mondays. Let the kids help figure out how to pay the bills. Do family projects. Just forget the lesson manual for a while. All that talk about fathers and family and priesthood."

Kristin's sense of humor rescued her about the time Lona Larsen, the chorister, dramatically declared that all men are created equal and the Blazer boys sang "Give Me Some Men Who Are Stout-Hearted Men." "Give them to *me*," Kristin muttered. When the older girls explained how they were learning to be cheerful, care for children, and cook, knit, and crochet to prepare for the future, Kristin's headache blossomed despite her determination to take it all lightly.

"Get mad," she whispered to Megan. "This is a major put down. Not to mention false propaganda."

But Megan was leaning her head against her hand, her elbow propped on the corner of the bench. Her other hand was clenched.

Then Heather's class of four- and five-year-olds gave verses about family life. Bonny's class stood to sing a song about the temple and about families living together forever. Megan straightened and watched her children proudly.

Suddenly, in the middle of the temple song, serious little Elinor put her white hands over her face and sat down.

As a low current rushed through the chapel, Kristin grabbed Megan's hand and held on, both of them keeping their shoulders straight and forward, their heads high.

That evening Megan reluctantly agreed to go for a walk with Kristin. Meg scarcely wanted to move anymore, Kristin had noticed. If she didn't watch out, her lethargy would begin to show. As they walked, Kristin talked business.

"So what do you have against having a garage sale?" she'd prodded. "Does Nancy object to having it next door to her Home and Garden?"

Megan flinched. "But I don't have much to sell. I feel so broke, even after my folks came to our rescue. It's hard to let anything go."

"Well, you can use the money, even if your folks let you live on your inheritance for a couple of years. I wish I had one," Kristin lied. "Even with that, though, you've got to be practical. What about that workshop full of Richard's tools? Those ought to bring some cash."

"But they're his tools."

Two steps later Kristin felt the shock. "You think he's coming back," she breathed. "You really think he's going to come home. Oh, Meg!"

Megan said nothing, just kept walking until Kristin caught up and pulled her down on the grass beside her. Megan was breathing a little hard and they'd only walked three blocks. "Megan, do you seriously think he's going to walk in one day and say, 'Hey, Meg, I forgot my tools'?"

Megan managed a tight smile. "Nutmeg, not Meg. He came up with Nutmeg on our honeymoon when I was being silly." She looked away, and Kristin gave her time.

"Oh, I guess I don't think so. Maybe I do. I don't know. I think he's alive, Kris. Something might bring him back. One of the kids might get sick. Becky's going to graduate in a couple of years. I used to think that he'd come back when the baby was born . . . "

Megan's fantasies sprawled nakedly before them on the grass. Kristin could have wept. Finally, she said, "How could he ever look you in the eye?"

"There's still a remote chance that there's a logical reason why he disappeared like that. Isn't there?"

"Like what?"

"Like being involved in something political. Or something illegal, like drugs or something. I don't know."

"*Richard*?"

"What do I really know about his life outside our

home? I just think that eventually something will bring him back."

"Such as reading in the Happy Ads that all his tools are for sale?"

They laughed then, truly laughed, picturing Richard's shocked, narrow face scanning the gritty tabloid. But where? At a laundromat? At a restaurant?

Then Megan stood up. "One thing I know. He *has* to come back, because I have to know why. If he doesn't, I'll have to bring him back somehow.

"A terrific reason for having a garage sale," Kristin said. That clinched it.

"Kris," Megan then said urgently. Kristin looked up, surprised by her tone. "Why did you tell my kids about Richard leaving? You know. The night I was sick."

"I thought they should know. You weren't in any condition to tell them. I thought maybe they'd help you more. You know how kids tend to blame their mothers for anything that goes wrong. Moms just aren't supposed to get sick."

"Or deserted."

"Right."

There was a pause. "I'm sorry if you wish I hadn't," Kristin began, but she could hear the defensiveness in her own voice. Megan shook her head and got up. She walked with her eyes on the horizon. They walked half a block in silence.

"If I could just get him out of my head," Megan said, in a voice as thin as the breeze in the maples. "I hear him talking in my head when I'm not thinking about anything in particular. I remember the shape of his hands, the way he'd tip his chin to kiss me. A million things you'd never think you notice."

"It'll go away."

"Will it, Kris? I don't know."

"Yes. Mostly." They slackened their pace a little. "I know the best cure, at least I've heard it's the best."

"What's that?"

"Find somebody else."

Megan winced. "Not me. All I'd do is compare. I feel battered as it is. All I need is another guy."

Kristin smiled. "I know what you mean. It's just . . . "

"What? You found someone?"

"No," Kristin said hurriedly, "there's just this doctor at the clinic. He's always been there, but suddenly he's *there*. Know what I mean?"

Megan stared at her as if she were about to disintegrate before her eyes.

"Hey, Meg, it's all right. I'm not going to elope. He just got divorced and probably doesn't want to get involved anyway."

"But you feel different," Megan insisted, stopping in front of her walk. "That's what you're saying, isn't it?"

Kristin shrugged. "I guess so."

Megan's eyes were dark-rimmed, her mouth unsure. "See you," Kristin said and broke into a fast jog.

MEGAN

The children thought the garage sale was a wonderful idea, especially when they realized they could keep the profit from their own things. They were all beginning to need clothes. Magazines, candy bars, football cards, and paper dolls had become luxuries since their allowances had vanished with their father.

Scott brought a huge box from the basement and set it in the center of the family room floor. Then they scurried to their rooms to sort through their belongings. But the pile in the box rose only by fits and starts. "I'll take that book," Elinor cried nearly every time Becky or Scott dropped one in.

"You promised me that doll when you grew out of it," Heather fretted, peering over the side at Elinor's grimy child.

But Megan found she was the worst. She'd hunted through five stores before she'd found that light blue parka that flattered Scott's eyes. True, it was too small now, and he was the only boy in the family, but how could he drop it into the box without a second glance? And the ballet shoes Becky had worn in recitals. Megan and Richard had applauded from the first row until their hands ached. And the Barbie doll that had kept Becky and Megan sewing diminutive clothes for three summers. Could that be sold?

Then there was Elinor's blue-striped sailor dress. She'd worn it out to dinner on her fifth birthday, marching along with one hand in Megan's hand and the other in Richard's. Megan pulled out Heather's rubber-footed pajamas to save for the baby before she remembered they wouldn't be needed.

Finally she slipped off to the bathroom to splash cold water on her face and blow her nose hard. She was preparing to barter away their happy nest.

Megan promised herself that once the children finished she'd send them to the park, close her eyes, hold her breath so she wouldn't sniff Richard's cologne, and gather up his clothes. She would save only the royal blue robe she still wore to bed some nights and the engraved cufflinks she was keeping for Scott.

Meanwhile she had to find the key to the workshop. She'd never had a copy on her key ring. She'd checked the shop when Richard disappeared, entering it through the unlocked laundry room door. Illogically, she'd almost expected to find him there, asleep on the workbench, exhausted by some secret project. Or sulking. Any mood was fine. But the shop had echoed his absence as had no room in the house. Unable, or unwilling, to confront the ghosts he'd left behind, Megan had fled, locking the laundry room door behind her. And Richard had the only key.

Years ago she'd visited the workshop often, admiring the puzzles that came from the jigsaw ready for sanding. She'd idly nibble the rough corner on a pine scrap as she told Richard about Becky's day at kindergarten or her own attempts to toilet train Scott. She clearly remembered his listening, slightly preoccupied face, his long fingers sanding as he chuckled. Some of their closest moments had been in that shop, she thought now. But they'd been frequently interrupted. She'd have to check the baby or answer the phone, heard faintly through the wall.

In those days, they'd talked of how Scott could help Richard when he grew older. But when that time came, Richard didn't work in the shop much. Becky and Elinor each had a doll crib and a cupboard with their names stenciled on the fronts. But when Heather turned two, Richard had simply repainted Becky's outgrown furniture and stenciled HEATHER.

Megan thought there must be an extra key in the oak desk where they kept bills and bank statements, but after going through the drawers and cubbyholes twice, she gave up. Next she hunted through the places he might stick an extra key — places she didn't inspect often enough to remember seeing one. Once calling a locksmith would have been the solution. Now she didn't even consider it.

The refrigerator top had only a small bag of potato chips pushed too far back to be seen from below, a big plate of dust-covered artificial fruit, and gritty stamps she'd saved for Scott's album. She wiped the stamps on her jeans and took them to Scott's room.

Next she checked the wide-mouthed vase on the sill above the sink, sorting paper clips, bobby pins, and ballpoint pens. That reminded her of the leather box on the dresser. There Richard kept his change, tie clips, and receipts. At the bottom of the box she found not just the shop key, but Richard's key ring.

Megan sat down carefully on the edge of the bed. Richard's house key, car keys, office key, the key to the workshop, and the garage key were all there. All these weeks they'd lain secret at the bottom of the leather box she'd given him for their third wedding anniversary. Had he thought of that when he dropped them in that morning? Had he hidden them? Or had their weight gradually drawn them through the litter of everyday life? Had he considered taking the box with him? Did anything he left behind hurt him at all?

Megan believed old bones moved her body out the back door to the workshop. She had grown slack and bloated since her miscarriage. Pimples followed one another on to her forehead, and she felt greasy under her tongue, behind her eyelids, along the creases of her flesh. Everything she ate tasted faintly of mold. But still she ate.

And she forgot to feed Richard's fish in the aquarium. Remembering, she'd feed them extra. This morning she'd found the last swelled body floating just below the glass. With Scott's help, and under his accusing eyes, she'd poured the fish and water down the toilet.

Letting the fish die was a sin. But, she realized, she was no longer surprised to find herself capable of it.

She avoided her own reflection now. When she did see herself in the mirror, she stared, amused at how little she had changed. She looked so much more normal than she felt. Not caring for her body was not a sin. Nothing she needed to do required her to be attractive or even energetic. Her breasts, her womb, her slender legs, the confident tilt of her head — so what, she thought. Her body had defaulted already.

She put the key into the lock with an eerie sense of having turned into Richard. But once the door was opened, she knew she was herself, for Richard's presence rushed toward her in a gust. She steadied herself against the door frame. Richard's tools, dustier than the fruit on the refrigerator, seemed to buzz faintly with an echo of his nervous energy.

Then someone brushed by her. Scott looked around wildly. "What are you doing in here?" he accused. "This stuff is Dad's. You have no rights in here."

She realized he had hoped, irrationally, that his father was here when he saw the open door. She both wanted to hug him and to slap him. "We need the money, Scott. Don't be mad at me. I didn't leave you."

He brushed her roughly as he ran out the door.

When Megan drove the loaded station wagon over to Kristin's, the absence of Richard's leather-working kit nagged at her. It would have been a good item to sell. She'd wondered if Scott had kept it for himself, but he swore he hadn't seen it and she believed him. He must know she'd let him keep it if he wanted it.

As Kristin applauded, they unloaded the aquarium,

some of Richard's tools (Megan had kept the hammers, paint-brushes, and the jigsaw and sander), wedding presents they'd never used, even a set of wildly-printed purple sheets, still wrapped in plastic.

When they drove back home again, Megan was as jubilant as the children. They fixed a quick dinner of hot dogs and pork and beans, then she called Nancy and told her three of the bridesmaids' dresses were completed. She'd finished them at midnight, but she hadn't wanted Nancy to know about the garage sale.

Nancy rushed over, brimming with compliments and gratitude. She sat down for a few minutes to chat.

"You're really a lifesaver, Megan. I knew I'd be busy this week planning the Relief Society luncheon, but I didn't know I was in for such a shock."

"What happened?"

"Well, I probably shouldn't tell you, but you'll know tomorrow anyway. Tuesday night the bishop asked me to be the new Relief Society president."

"Congratulations! You'll be great."

"Thanks, but I really feel overwhelmed. Actually, I'm glad I got the chance to tell you this, because I want you to know that I asked for you to be one of my counselors. First thing."

Megan raised her eyebrows politely, and her heart beat faster. Still, she cautioned herself, she hadn't heard from the bishop, and obviously Nancy would be sustained at church tomorrow.

"Well, the bishop felt it wasn't a good idea," Nancy

added. "He thought that it would be too hard on you right now."

Megan swallowed. "Oh, that's all right. I wouldn't have expected you to even ask for me."

"Of course I would. I just wanted you to know that." Megan could hardly wait for Nancy to finish thanking her and sweep out the door with the dresses. Then she dropped on to the sofa, trembling from exhaustion and from the sense of being wrongly accused.

The next night, for the second Sunday evening in a row, the Stevens children played outside until dark as if there were no one at home to call them in. Finally Becky got off the telephone long enough to call them, but only after darkness blackened all the windows. Even then they were keyed up, reluctant to settle down and go to bed.

Megan heard them from the bedroom and put a pillow over her head. Even in the darkness the sequence with the bishop that afternoon repeated itself. She had stopped him as he hurried past her toward his office. She'd asked him if he thought she was unworthy in some way. His kind face had grown concerned, then, she'd thought, a little wary. Of course not, he'd said.

She'd told him of her conversation with Nancy. "I just had to be sure you don't think I've done something . . . wrong."

He'd paused, rocking back on his heels as if she'd just gained his full attention. "Of course I can't reveal if that conversation with Nancy actually took place, just as I consider this conversation confidential. But I don't have any doubts about your worthiness. Maybe we haven't been as supportive as we should be, Sister Stevens, but I don't think we should overload you with work either."

Then Megan had gone into the chapel and watched as Janet Madsen, who, the congregation was told, had six children, one just ten days old, was sustained as first counselor, and as Aurora Jones, a grandmother who specialized in crafts, was sustained as second counselor.

Now, beneath her shelter of pillows, Megan imagined herself seated on a bucket, her hands gripping a rope. She sank slowly, gracefully into a well. Silence grew as she floated downward. Noise from the children only sank her deeper until everything, even her mind was still.

The next morning, light at Becky's voice over her ear brought her almost to ground level. "I'm sick," she muttered and sank again.

Once or twice the children caught her stumbling back to bed after going to the bathroom. They'd never seen her so disheveled, shaky, and blank-eyed.

"Oh, Mom," Becky said, "you must really have the flu. Shall I call Kristin?"

"Who?" Megan croaked. "Oh, no, she's at work. Fix some peanut butter sandwiches." She went back to bed.

On Tuesday morning she reached the bottom of the well, a place soft, plush, and utterly empty, like black snow. There she found a clarity she hadn't discovered on her way down. Even with her eyes closed, blankets clutched around her face, and sunk into herself as far as she could go, Megan felt herself within an opening.

"Do you want to die?" she heard herself ask, respectfully. She waited as the question reverberated gently. The darkness caressed her face like a loving hand. It soothed her nostrils, her lungs, stroked her flesh as if she were infinitely precious. Dark cushioned her ears.

She was surprised, even then, that no fear of God or judgment decided the question. There were no terrors here, nothing like what waited at the top of the well. The thought of meeting Paula again brought tears. Paula would understand. Anyone who knew her well would understand.

Becky, Scott, Elinor, and Heather at the top of the well didn't settle the question either. It seemed clear they'd be better off without her. From this safe nucleus, Megan could see herself clearly — so inadequate, so sad.

Thinking this, she seemed to be both at the top of the well looking in and at the bottom peacefully considering her fate.

Then an answer began forming deep in her solar plexus, hard and unmistakable. No, I want to live; she considered this. She almost smiled when she understood that her reason was curiosity. She wanted to see how everything turned out. Drawing a deep breath, she gave the rope a tug so that the Megan at the top would start to pull her out.

Daylight stung her eyes. She was weak from hunger and wanted the bathroom, the kitchen, and, yes, her bed, all at once. The kitchen seemed coated with margarine, crumbs, and something sticky that might be dried orange juice. She sat at the table, her head in her hands, as the children rioted around her.

Scott needed clean jeans so he could go on a scouting trip. Becky was tired of her siblings and wanted to visit friends. Heather was determined to sit on Megan's lap, and

Elinor stood behind her, pulling a comb through her mother's matted hair.

Something flat and colorful lay before her on the table. "Kristin brought that by on her way to work," Elinor said. "She's coming back tonight to see how you are."

Megan looked at the red, green, blue, and violet letters and shapes. She saw that it was the cover of a pamphlet. She closed her eyes for a minute and rubbed her fingers over them. She tried again to read the cover, as if doing so would solve the jagged morning. "Autumn Quarter," she said aloud.

"Oh, that. It's a class catalog, Mother," Becky explained, spinning by, exasperated by Megan's dullness.

"Yes," Megan said, turning the small booklet over in her hands.

ELINOR

Elinor closed the door to her room one Saturday evening with a sense of relief. Heather had gone with their mother to the store, so, for a while, Elinor was alone. Of course, even when Heather was there, her childish murmuring to her dolls and the click of plastic dishes was unobtrusive, even mildly comforting. Heather was so young she assumed playing with pencils was the usual thing for older sisters to do.

But Elinor knew it was not. She sat on the pale green carpet, surrounded by pencils. Many were from the original lot she'd heisted from the buffet drawer when she was even younger than Heather. Her mother had carried them back that evening, but soon they were gone again. Finally, Elinor told her mother, "These aren't pencils. They're people."

Her mother was so surprised she let the pencils stay, and with satisfaction Elinor heard her repeat the comment

to her father. Soon there were writing pencils in the drawer
and Elinor's pencils in a shoe box under her bed. Fifty-three
of them now. Occasionally she raided the drawer for a pencil with unusual promise, and it was seldom missed. To
everyone else, pencils were interchangeable.

They laughed when Elinor scoured the house searching for a missing pencil-kid. She still mourned the loss of
Scarlet and believed that Becky had carelessly picked her up
one day, then lost her at school. Becky refused to even discuss it. Scott would pay some attention, but not Becky.

Elinor gathered that her parents thought she'd soon
tire of playing with pencils. But now she had them organized into groups in a boarding school, and the reading and
spelling groups she'd copied from school had transformed.

Beside her right foot lay the cartwheelers, next to
them the line-drawers, and to their left the twirlers. Blue
Michaela, her favorite, was the head twirler, but she had
gotten the post through honest auditions, not favoritism.

The boarding school's competitions, feuds, and mys-
teries took most of Elinor's pencil playing time. She brought
home squalls from school and introduced plots from television shows. There was nothing the pencils couldn't do. Their
very facelessness gave them character and versatility.

But sometimes, like this evening when Heather was
gone to the store with Mother, Elinor played the game she'd
begun after the Bad Time.

One of the pencils, an important one, disappeared.
He might be a teacher or the soccer coach. (A few adult
pencils were kept in the box for such roles, for ordinarily
Elinor preferred playing with children.)

Blue Michaela always organized the search and found the missing person under the dresser, against the wall, under the bed. Or once, after an extraordinarily complicated story that took three days, he was discovered at the bottom of Elinor's winter boot. He might be sick, injured, held captive by bandits, or trapped by Russians who thought he was a spy.

Sometimes Elinor wearied at that point and had Blue Michaela simply announce, "He explained it all to the police (or to the doctor)," getting the tedious logic out of the way and jumping to the happy reunion.

She had played the game often during the first part of the summer. The game helped her escape Becky's storms and Scott's silence, which contained something so cold it made freezing spiders run down her neck. Elinor couldn't bear to watch Mother trying to be patient but looking as if she would shatter at any second. Elinor didn't see how Becky and Scott could be so awful. When Heather cried at night, Elinor sped across the room, too fast for the dark to snatch her, and held Heather's chubby body in her arms until they both fell asleep.

When Elinor herself woke up from terrible nightmares she could never quite remember, she trotted on trembling legs to Mother's bed, and her mother pulled her close just like when Elinor snuggled Heather. She didn't suppose Becky or Scott could do that.

One day when things were particularly dreadful, she made a flat number 3 out of salt dough, mounted it on heavy cardboard, then let it lie on her window sill for a week. When it was dry, she painted it green with her poster

paints and let it dry again. Then she took four thumbtacks
and hammered it to the outside of her door.

"What makes you think you live in a separate
apartment?" Becky had asked.

"It doesn't make sense," Scott said. "Yours is the
fourth room from the front door and the fifth from the back.
Didn't you count?"

"Counting has nothing to do with it," Elinor said. "I
intend to live in Room 3." She thought the reason should be
obvious.

Now she didn't play with the pencils so often because
she was busy helping her mother change Daddy's workshop
into a nursery school. Mother needed her, too. She could
see that.

Elinor came out of her room one day to find her
mother standing in the center of the empty workshop, turning slowly. "What do you think, Elinor? If you were three or
four again, what would you want on the walls?"

So they put up shiny plastic on one wall, the kind
you use on charts, Mother said, right over the fresh, pale
yellow paint. The kids could draw on it with washable mark-
ers, then wipe it all off and do it again. She and Heather
immediately did a Christmas mural to cool them in the
August heat.

Then, after a talk sitting cross-legged on the floor
with a box of raisins between them, she and Mother decided
to put burlap on the opposite wall. Scott had helped staple
it on.

Elinor had been surprised that Scott would help at
all. He'd been furious when Mother sold some of Daddy's

tools. When Scott found out, he'd stormed into Elinor's room. He kicked her pencils across the floor by accident but was too upset to apologize.

"She's selling Dad's stuff!" he'd said, his voice so terrible it was a scream, although Elinor could barely hear it. "She's glad he's gone."

Elinor shook her head. Her voice wouldn't work, and she felt her stomach begin to tremble.

"She is! When he comes home, what'll he think? We ought to go in her bedroom and burn up her closet!"

Then his face had crumpled and he sprawled across her bed, sobbing into Harry's furry belly. Elinor had regrouped her pencils, then scooted closer to the bed and rubbed his leg as if he had a muscle cramp.

Only Elinor knew that Scott had taken all his savings to the yard sale at Kristin's house, intending to buy back everything of his father's. But maybe he hadn't had enough money. Or maybe, with Mother and Kristin being so businesslike and cheerful, he'd lost his nerve. Elinor had watched him out of the corners of her eyes. He stood rigidly as a man in a tweed sport coat bought the large drill and as a smart-alecky high school boy paid for the aquarium. Elinor wanted to touch Scott or take his hand, but she knew better.

Now he was often gone to scout meetings, swimming with his deacon's quorum, camping with his scout leader's family. People seemed to think Scott needed fun more than Becky and Heather and Elinor did.

Still, Scott had stapled the burlap that afternoon, chatting about how the children could pin their art work to it. He asked Mother a lot of questions about how much money she thought she could make.

Once, when Elinor had her back turned, he gave her a hard tickle on both sides of her ribs.

Only Becky had refused to be drawn into their preparations. "Nice," she said occasionally, but only when she had to poke her strawberry curls in the door to ask Mother's permission to go somewhere. None of her friends' mothers worked, and now some of their little brothers and sisters might come here to nursery school.

"It's mortifying!" she'd yelled the day they started painting the walls.

"You're mortifying!" Elinor had shouted back. She hadn't known what it meant exactly, but she like the sound of it. Flung back at Becky, the word had made her sweep out of the workshop like an offended princess, leaving mother holding her wet, paint-smeared hands in the air.

"Elinor!" Mother said reprovingly, but then she giggled and so did Elinor.

Now three children in the ward were registered for half a day when school began. Mother hoped there would be more. She had to go to school at night for a while before they could really call it a nursery school, she said.

But it already had a name. Scott had been stenciling the letters on wood to paint in brown enamel while Mother and Elinor carefully painted scalloped shutters beside the windows outside. THE GINGERBREAD HOUSE, the sign said. Elinor had blurted the name as they walked round and round what used to be the workshop. When Mother hugged

her and started talking about shutters and petunias, Elinor
felt like crying with pride.

This Saturday evening Elinor decided to let an orange
boy pencil help Blue Michaela organize the search for the
missing scout leader. But just as she'd thought out the plot
and gotten the characters chosen, her energy flagged. She
went to the window and stared out at the darkness for a long
time until she saw Mother's car pull into the driveway and
heard Heather's chirpy voice float out the car window.

That sent her back to pick up the tall blue pencil
selected to disappear. Carefully, she rolled him under a loose
molding at the head of Heather's bed. Then she sat there,
looking at the dark line that held him. Her stomach felt
wormy, and the center of her forehead buzzed as if it were
about to get bumped.

"Don't think we're coming for you unless you make
some effort to be found," she said at last, then gathered up
the other pencils before Heather could bounce into the room.

10

BECKY

Of course they had to kidnap her the first day of school. That was a drill team tradition. If you'd been chosen for the junior varsity drill team a couple of senior varsity girls would burst into your bedroom, wake you with the team song, and pull you out of bed.

If Mom thought this was bad, what about five years ago when they dragged the girls out to breakfast in their nightgowns? Now they sat and talked while you put yourself together.

Any time before this year, Mom would have understood. She would have thought it charming. She wouldn't mind getting up early and putting on her blue duster with the eyelet trim to let the girls in so Becky could be properly surprised in bed. It wouldn't matter if Kim and Alison, both seniors, and Heidi, a junior like Becky, woke the girls when they thundered and screeched down the hall.

But right now, of course, everything was a big crisis. Mom had even tried to hush them as they screamed the song into Becky's ears. As if Mom didn't know Becky would be dying in her bed if she hadn't heard the song that morning and known after so much wondering if she'd made it. Dozens of girls, the unchosen, were waking up in empty bedrooms. Still, Mom had practically slammed Becky's bedroom door behind her.

The intrusion bugged Mom like heck, and that made Becky furious. How could her mother crawl out of bed looking like a pile of dirty laundry and silently open the front door to the excited faces of three of the most popular girls in school? Besides, Alison had a tongue like a knife, and after last year the thing Becky needed least was more talk about her family.

Why didn't Mom just hang a sign on the front porch reading, THE ABANDONED? Anyone could tell by the front lawn that got too long before Mom noticed and remembered to tell Scott to stay home and cut it. You couldn't live on a street like this without paying attention to detail.

Detail was what Becky watched this morning, despite the girls' clamor behind her. Let them wait. Her hair was just right now, the golden-red curls cascading back from her face. Her eyes dazzled, outlined with blue, lightly shadowed. Now a hint of blush over her cheekbones, and the lipstick that set off her lavender sweater.

"Oh, she's not," Becky heard Heidi moan and tuned into the conversation. Even before she knew who to feel sorry for, she was glad they had a new scandal to discuss.

The Becky-Stevens's-father-disappeared story had, hopefully, died during the long, disorganized, boring summer.

"Who's not what?" She tipped her head so that the curls tumbled to the right. She pretended to look past her own reflection to Heidi's petite figure curled on her unmade bed.

"Michelle. Pregnant. And she is."

"You're kidding." Becky grabbed her jacket (a year old now) and picked up her purse. "That's awful."

"I don't suppose she'll be doing anything about it," Alison said as they headed down the hall. Kim shrugged, and Becky and Heidi exchanged glances.

Becky saw Heather watching from her bed and waved as they passed her. Elinor had her back turned. "Bye, Mom," Becky called just as her hand touched the doorknob. No need to hurry out, Mom. I'm gone.

"Into the wreck," Kim said. Her midnight blue Datsun gleamed beside the curb.

Becky ran her hand over the seat covers in back and tried to imagine Kim or Michelle or anyone, even herself, making love in a back seat. It seemed so awkward. No boy had ever asked her to get in the back seat.

"Okay, Becky," Alison said once they were on the main road, "before we get to Sambo's we've got to tell you something. See, we don't tell everybody this."

Heidi's knee bumped Becky's. Did she already know?

"We have to let a lot of girls into drill team, you know? But within the team there's a special club. We'll be choosing the junior members soon, and we want you and

Heidi. Believe me, being a junior member is a big honor. It means you're virtually set for your last year."

Becky felt the pressure on her knee increase slightly. "What do we have to do? Try out or something?"

"Not formally." Alison looked at Kim and they giggled. "A lot of it is just desire." They laughed again.

"Well, you've got it then," Becky said, trying not to sound too eager. She was embarrassed when the girls in the front seat kept laughing, then relieved when Kim pulled into a parking place and everybody jumped out.

Heidi let her in on the secret when they were walking home from school, worn out. Becky's cheeks ached from smiling so much. She was glad Heidi's boy friend, Lance, had football practice after school. That gave them some time alone.

"What they do," Heidi explained slowly, "is to divide the whole drill team into virgins and vamps. Not real virgins and vamps. Those are just the basic names. A virgin is a girl who's mainly untouched. You know. And a vamp is somebody who's been around. You can't be in the club if you're a virgin."

Becky swallowed hard, then laughed and shook her curls. "So how do they define a virgin?"

"There are these guys who hang out with the girls in the club. You know, that whole bunch."

Becky nodded. Lance was one of them, but not a ringleader.

"One of them has to vouch for you. He says you're not a virgin except maybe technically. Technically is okay. Like maybe she's done a lot but not the real thing."

Becky was silent.

"Hey, don't worry. Who cares about their club, anyway?"

They kept walking. Becky stared at the leaves, green and yellow against the bright September sky. She thought she would remember those leaves forever. Finally she said, "What are you going to do?"

"It's easy for me," Heidi said. "If you want to be in the club, I'll be in it, too. Lance can tell them I'm okay, and they'll never really know what that means. He's my boy friend after all."

But I don't have one, Becky thought. "I don't suppose Craig would qualify."

Heidi laughed. "I know you went with him half of last year, Bec, but somehow I don't think they're going to believe the seminary president on something like this."

"It wouldn't be true anyway," Becky said.

They stopped and faced each other. Becky felt Heidi was the one person who really knew her. That gamine face under the dark curls listened to all her secrets eventually. Heidi was Catholic. She wore a cross every day, and for a long time Becky had tried to convert her. She didn't convert, but she did stay Becky's friend. In spite of Becky's recent moods, despite the crowd at the ward who didn't think she should hang around with a Catholic and didn't mind letting either of them know, in spite of Becky's father disappearing, Heidi was solid.

"Hey, don't Bec. I don't care if we join the damn thing anyway."

Becky set down her books and wiped her cheeks

with both hands. "I know you don't. Listen, Heidi, you're my best friend. You know that?"

"Sure. We don't need that bunch anyway. We're on the drill team, right? I mean, who do we have to impress?"

"That's easy for you to say," Becky huffed, but made it a joke. "You've got a boy friend on the football team and he thinks you're terrific."

"I guess I wouldn't be too surprised if we got married someday," Heidi said thoughtfully. "Coming to my house for a while?"

"I don't think so. Mom's probably freaking out now because I'm late. I'll see you tomorrow."

That night, lying awake in her room, Becky had an imaginary conversation with her mother about joining the inner circle and what she'd have to do to get there.

"You probably think I've already done all that," Becky said.

Her mother looked injured. "Becky, of course I don't."

"Well, I've kissed boys and necked with a few of them." When her mother's eyes widened, she added, "And I like it. You might have been sweet sixteen, but I'm not. Besides, I don't even have to go all the way. Just far enough."

She rolled on to her back and stared at her pale blue ceiling. I'll never get to sleep, she thought. Her mind wandered through the day, then she found herself unexpectedly talking with her father.

"It's not like you to think of selling yourself," he was saying in his grave way, when his eyebrows quirked upward but his mouth grew lines at each side. "And what a prize—

just getting to associate more closely with other girls who have done the same."

Becky felt the color rise in her face in the dark room.

"It's not like that," she said hotly. "I might have known you'd see it that way. I like lots of those boys. There are a couple I like a lot. That's the only way I'd go through with it." There was a pause. Then Dad reached over and took both her hands in his. "Don't do it, Bec. You've just turned sixteen. Trust me on this one. You'll be glad if you do." His familiar hands tightened on hers, and she felt in his fingers a strength she suddenly missed.

She heard a gasp and opened her eyes to find her face flooded with tears. She rolled flat on her stomach and wept. Finally she sat up, blew her nose on a tissue from the box near her bed, and walked over to the window. The streetlight on the corner looked like a narrow face under a golf cap.

"You left me," she told it silently. "You deserve everything I do. I have to have something, too."

Courtney was cute, blond, and tan, with the sun-bleached eyebrows and lashes Becky had always found irresistible. His way of glancing at her sideways, just a flash of dark blue between fair fringes, fired a flame in the pit of her stomach. Last year he'd given her nothing more than a smile whose meaning depended on whether his popularity was by design or accident. But now he was turning up by her locker or bumping into her between classes.

"Hi," he'd say with that sideways glance. They'd walk, their arms grazing, their eyes meeting between Becky's bright comments. He didn't say much, but Becky had grown used to seeing him for several five-minute spaces per day, then to hearing his voice on the telephone at night. In some ways the telephone was better. Then he almost had to talk, so gradually they got to know each other.

When Court asked her to the Harvest Ball, she was happy and unsurprised. She arranged to sleep at Heidi's house the night before the dance so they could manicure their nails and wash and set their hair the next morning.

"Of course I have to wear my old green dress," Becky said, waving her right hand so Heidi could admire her dull pink nails.

"Your apple green? Bec, you look devastating in that."

"Thanks. But everyone's going to remember it from last year's Christmas Dance."

"No, they won't. Court won't. That's who counts, isn't it?"

"You'll look perfect in apricot. But Alison will probably strut up to me in that black thing she's been crowing about and say, 'Becky, you *always* look so *cute* in that dress.' "

Heidi choked, then burst out laughing. Becky joined her. "She is pretty awful," Heidi said. "Wonder why she's so popular?"

"Anyone that caustic has to be popular," Becky said. "Everyone's afraid of her."

"I guess so. Lance doesn't like her. He'd hardly even talk to her about their club. Hey, I wanted to double tonight, but I get the feeling the guys don't want to."

"Really? I didn't hear anything about it," Becky lied. Last night Court had slid an arm around her at the 7-Eleven and whispered, "Let's not double with anyone." His lips had grazed hers before they went around the corner to the counter.

"Okay," she'd said, reaching up to kiss his chin to keep things even.

That night she tingled again. They slid into his father's LTD, and he pulled her over with his right arm. He kissed her hair before he started the car, then held her hand as he drove.

She danced in a haze of happiness in Court's arms. She talked, nibbled at refreshments, rushed through a conversation with Heidi in the gym bathroom, but it was all an excited blur. Again and again, they danced, Court's hands pressed lightly against her back, his heart thumping against her hand flat on his chest. She felt she was watching herself in a movie, as the evening unfolded, fascinated to see what would happen next and savoring every second.

"Where would you like to eat?" he asked afterward. "Anywhere," she said. He smiled and drove to a small French restaurant in Salt Lake. They both ordered the quiche, ate quickly, then the strawberry tortes, and ate slowly.

"You're very pretty," Court said, setting his fork neatly beside his plate.

"I really had a good time tonight," Becky smiled.

"Come on," he said, digging in his pocket with one hand, picking up the bill with the other. He glanced back sideways as he stood.

I love you, Becky thought suddenly, surprising herself. She wouldn't tell him, though, not until she was absolutely positive he felt the same way.

Court pulled off the freeway at the first Bountiful

exit, but before they reached Orchard Drive, he turned down a dark side street and stopped the car. Becky waited, her heart thundering. When he reached for her, she came into his arms. Their lips touched and held.

"Let's get in the back," he whispered after a few minutes of lovely, drowning kisses. "Leave your dress here so we don't ruin it." He pulled down the back zipper.

"Wait," Becky started, but as he kissed her again his fingers touched the skin of her back so gently and confidently that she could only tighten her arms around his shoulders. She felt some clenched part of her, deep inside, loosen and relax.

"Nice," Court said, helping her lift off her dress. "Know what? I really like you."

So easy to slip into the back seat, then she was in his arms again, more magically lost than when they were dancing. Every place he touched seemed smooth and glowing. She felt her flesh rise to meet his hands, his lips. Her hands ran along his smooth, hard arms and back with wonder and pleasure. The magic went on and on. But when she felt his hand slip inside her panties, she froze. Suddenly the interior of the car came into focus. Headlights skimmed through their windows like prying eyes. She heard his breath, rough and fast, and almost laughed, embarrassed. His hand reached lower. Her foot was starting to cramp painfully.

"Court," she said, struggling to sit up. His left hand pushed flat on her collarbone, his mouth covered her mouth hard until she thought she would gag. As she turned her head slightly, finding air, she felt his thumb jab so hard and heedlessly that hurt streaked to her core. Now her hand, resting against his face, was resisting, her mouth moved under his only asking to finish up; but he sighed and continued, his tongue seeking hers. She felt her warm tears slide into her ears one after another. She stared at the square light fixture on the leather ceiling, feeling helpless and ridiculous.

Finally Court drew a long breath. She felt his right hand withdraw as he planted a wet kiss on the tip of her nose. Becky's chest ached when he next moved his left hand, which had supported his weight. Inconspicuously, she drew her hands up the sides of her face to catch her tears, then smoothed the wetness along the hair over her ears and shook out her curls. Court cleared his throat. When he reached into his pocket for a handkerchief, she saw a dark streak across his hand.

Becky felt her cheeks flame in the dark car.

"Guess you're in," he said, glancing at her.

She tried to find a steady tone. "They ask for proof?"

"Of course not. What's the matter?"

She looked at him straight on, and in a second he reached out and carressed her hair. She tried to smile and began rearranging her clothes. When she looked back at him, his hair mussed, his eyes watchful, she couldn't help reaching for him. He kissed her—a nice, warm kiss—and pulled her close.

"I meant it, Bec. You're a very pretty girl."

She stayed a minute in the warm crook of his arm. She wanted to cry and let him gather her in like an orphan, but she bit her lip instead until she tasted blood. Passing headlights silvered them both.

"Maybe I'd better put on my dress."

"Right." He helped her lift it over her shoulders and lower it gently in the cramped back seat. "Ready?" he asked lightly and zipped it up.

"A true gentleman," she teased, reaching for her evening bag in hopes the small comb and lipstick she'd tossed in could repair most of the damage. If he heard the irony in her voice, he chose not to answer.

MEGAN

Cruising. That's what the kids called it when they dragged the main roads, looking for fun. That's what it felt like when Megan floated along the day's surface like a raft on water deep enough to cover the rocks, the snags along the way.

All through August and much of September, Megan cruised. Things got done or they didn't. Gingerbread House did. Corkboard went up. Plastic went up. Paint. Shutters. Meals sometimes got cooked and sometimes didn't. Laundry piled up until she noticed and finally Becky and Scott started doing their own. Megan congratulated them. Who had ever said she had to control every little thing in the house? Had she really, anyway? Or was it an illusion?

Now The Gingerbread House was becoming a reality. Children appeared at its door every morning, hammering with little fists until Megan hurried through the laundry room, closing the door behind her, and opened the door that faced the driveway. She wished she could keep Elinor out of school to help, but Elinor rushed home anyway and stayed with the afternoon session until they left at a quarter past four.

The children Megan cared for were concerned about sharing the chalk fairly and how many graham crackers each could eat during snack period. They looked into Megan's face earnestly but without judgment. They patted her cheeks with sticky fingers and occasionally one grabbed her in a hug around the legs. She worked hard but felt an ease, like a runner resting in her stride. Her mind was as busy as her body, at least for now.

Evenings she went walking with Kristin or to class. Since Kristin had badgered her to sign up for an evening class, Megan had found Sociology of the Family, meeting at the high school Tuesday and Thursday evenings. It would count toward renewing her certificate.

She and Kristin walked Mondays and Wednesdays, and on Fridays she and whichever children were home played board games. Monopoly. Life. Careers. Scrabble. Chinese Checkers. Night after night she paid herself her bonus for cruising through the day. She crawled into her empty bed and listened as the house gradually quieted and went to sleep. Then she had the luxury of lying in darkness with no one to see her and check by her eyes, her skin, the muscles of her face and body, how she was *really* doing. She knew. She was doing fine. She just felt lousy.

Alone, she could feel. She tried to empty her mind

of all the explanations, arguments, rationalizations, and accusations. She let her feelings assail her, unprotected, until she fell asleep.

Compared with her private confrontations, the evening class often seemed tame. There were eight women enrolled, most about Megan's age or older. The teacher, Alan Goldmun, was a counselor at a drug and alcohol center during the day and a teacher in the evening. Just for variety, he'd said. He'd told the class to call him Alan and taught perched on the front of the desk, his head cocked as he waited for the eight of them to discuss his questions. Megan thought he usually seemed a little disappointed.

We're rusty, she thought. None of us have been in a classroom for years. From the talk she heard before and after class, she had the feeling her fellow students were taking the class as a diversion. Only she seemed to have a professional interest. But the others so intimidated her with their clique, however superficial their thinking, that she never wanted to comment. Sometimes she felt Alan's eyes watching her react when someone said something particularly obvious.

One evening she had to attend Scott's Court of Honor before class. It would make her a few minutes late, but she hummed as she got ready. Heather splashed, chattering in the tub, while Megan combed her hair and put on lipstick. Megan watched her daughter's rounded body out of the corner of one eye and smiled. She was so unselfconscious. Megan still felt a pang when she remembered that Heather was the last baby, and hardly a baby at all. But the pang was slight tonight. More like the ache under a bird's wings, a bird on the far end of a branch sensing the first inkling of flight.

Later, she sat on a folding metal chair and watched Scott collect three merit badges. By the time she pulled into the parking lot next to the high school, her head ached. She turned off the ignition and wondered how she could have felt so . . . foreign.

For she had sat stiffly at the edge of the aisle feeling utterly apart from the room full of proud parents, a few of them holding babies. They were their friends—hers and Richard's. But now that Richard was gone, they didn't know what to say to her, where to look when their glances met. Neither did she.

And Scott. The pain tightened like a cord around her skull. He had barely glanced at her when he got his badges, just kissed her quickly, dutifully, then grinned at his scoutmaster, who threw an arm around him. Megan had kept her smile, swallowing her pain and guilt, and everyone in the room had smiled too, dabbing their eyes when Ed Browning pulled Scott in like a stray pup.

When she dropped Scott off at home, the headlights had caught Becky and her new boyfriend kissing at the edge of the porch. Becky's head was bent back, her arms high around his neck. His hands were planted firmly on Becky's rear, but quickly moved to her waist when the car swung close. Maybe the gleam of the headlights had burned the backs of his hands, Megan thought.

Megan walked rapidly toward the high school, although she was debating whether she should go back home. Then she'd see what was really going on. She could send

Court home, shoo the girls and Scott into bed, and take a nice, hot bath herself. But her shoes beat a steady rhythm to the school, and soon she was sliding into a desk. She felt less embarrassed when Alan stopped mid-sentence and smiled. Maybe he was glad she was there?

The class, it seemed, was discussing the traditional family and the women's movement. Megan crossed her ankles, leaned back, and listened. She wished Kristin were present. Kristin had a lot to say about a woman's earning power and the difficulty of collecting child support.

Now Alan was writing something on the board — the number of female-headed households in Utah, then the poverty rate. "See, a child who lives in a home with the mother at the head has six times the usual chance of living in poverty," he said.

Megan swallowed and thought of her children going back to school in last year's clothes. Next year nothing would fit. What would they do then? She could pass Elinor's things to Heather. But there was no one to hand things down to Becky or Scott. And by the time Elinor grew into Bec's clothes, they were hopelessly out of style.

She took a deep breath and remembered the Gingerbread House. She was, after all, working hard for that very reason. She raised her hand. "But how many of those women are on welfare?" She remembered the office she'd visited and shuddered.

"About half," Alan said. "That's one way of being poor. The other is working."

He handed out some pages of statistics that compared men's and women's wages versus educational levels.

Megan scanned the numbers and percentages, then looked out the window into the black night. Her headache wasn't improving listening to this. Her college education, it seemed, mattered far less than being born into pink booties.

Pat, the blond woman in a pale pink sweater and slacks, was commenting, "I'm not saying all these women are lazy. But isn't this because of the high divorce rate? Some women, when they can't be dependent on a man any more, just become dependent on the state, don't they?"

"Why aren't women more independent?" Alan asked.

There was a silence.

"Which of you here have had experience being independent? Let's talk about independence for a few minutes."

Instead they wanted to talk about partnership.

"But you're begging the question," Alan said. "What if the husband isn't there?"

Again, silence. Megan felt color rise in her face. She knew why these women couldn't discuss it. Such things happened to alien beings. Or to people who were clearly stupid, made dreadful mistakes, and were incapable of taking care of themselves.

She raised her hand. "Why don't women learn to be independent?"

Alan smiled. "Class?"

No one answered. Instead they looked at Megan. "Well," she answered slowly, wishing she hadn't asked the question, yet suddenly burning to talk, "I went right from my parents' home to my marriage. Didn't anyone else?"

Several women smiled and nodded.

"Now I'm on my own, at least for now," Megan continued. "My husband is missing."

They stared at her, then looked steadfastly at Alan as if Megan had thrown her clothes into the hall and was dancing naked before them. Pat cleared her throat.

"I think we're getting off the subject," she said.

"No," Alan replied, "I think we're finally coming close to the subject."

But Megan wouldn't look at him. She had already said too much. Alan stood up and went to the board again. He talked about fathers who didn't pay child support and women on welfare. He asked if anyone had ever seen movies about divorced or widowed fathers. Everyone had seen at least one. He got them to talk about what they'd seen.

"Why is it interesting to see the problems of single fathers?" he asked.

"The movies were so tender," June said. "It was very revealing to see how the father could learn to care for the child. I loved watching the feeling develop between father and child."

When they were tired of talking about the movies, Alan asked, "How many movies like that have you seen about single mothers?"

No one raised a hand. "Why not? Women are more likely to lose their jobs or to live in poverty. Isn't that more interesting?"

"No, not in the same way," Pat said at last, a little defensively. "We all know about those problems. Besides, in a movie like that the wife would just find another man. That's what the movie would be about."

"So it's interesting to watch men become fathers and to watch women get men," Alan said. "You may have something here, but I'm not sure what."

Megan didn't care. She only wanted class to end so she could escape into the dark parking lot again, the dark car, her own house on her own street, and into her own bed, with night behind the Priscilla curtains. She looked at the clock. She wished for the bell to ring ten minutes early.

When she looked back, Alan was watching her. To her surprise, he winked slightly and said, "Okay, let's call it a night. See you Thursday."

Megan pretended to fumble with her notebook and papers as the other women approached her desk by the door. She looked up when the pink outfit stopped beside her.

"It's so nice that you can come out to this class," Pat said. The others murmured. Then they swept by her, talking, and were gone.

Rage rose inside Megan, a rage she couldn't remember ever having felt, except maybe as a very young child. She gasped as the women's condescension hit her. She grabbed her notebook and purse and stepped into the aisle.

"Wow," someone said.

She looked back. Alan was watching her, arms folded across his knee propped up on a desk. "You won a scarlet letter tonight, didn't you?"

The rage was turning numb, but it was still there, burning like a smokeless fuel. "I guess I did. S for single? But I'm not. Maybe P for pathetic."

"How about just a D for different? To them, that is."

Megan took a deep breath. "Well," she said, "see you Thursday."

But in two quick steps he was at her side, opening the door for her. "You won't stop coming will you? I know I haven't gotten them to be the most responsive group, but I'd hate to see you drop the class."

He sounded sincere, even warm. "Oh, no, I'll keep coming. I need to renew my certificate in early childhood development."

"Where are you working?"

"I just opened a pre-school in what used to be my husband's workshop. We call it Gingerbread House."

He smiled. "How about a Coke or something? There a McDonald's next door here."

She shook her head but smiled back. "Please," he said.

Megan looked at him carefully while he ordered the drinks. She liked his curly dark hair. It looked like the kind of hair you'd never comb, just have cut and shaped. He was fairly tall, a rangy body with long arms and legs, olive skin with dark hair curling sparsely over his arms and at the neck of his open-collared shirt.

She watched his long fingers fumble with the plastic cap on his 7-Up. She stuck her straw through the slit in her own plastic cap and began to drink.

"I appreciate you sharing your situation with the class," he said, when he had the cap off. "I wish they'd been more receptive. They could have learned a lot from your experience."

Megan shrugged. "I guess it's not anything people

want to learn. I didn't, that's for sure. I wish I hadn't spoken up."

Alan frowned and shook his head. "Why not? Your experience is as valid as anyone else's."

Megan said nothing. She seldom drank Coke, but she was glad she'd ordered one. Her headache was dissipating now, just a little. She raised her eyebrows, shut her eyes, and bent her head all the way back.

"I've got some aspirin," Alan said.

"Do you always read minds?" she smiled as he reached into his back pocket and fished out a small tin. He shook out two aspirins and gave them to her. She swallowed the aspirins with her Coke.

He laughed. "That's reading a head, not a mind. No, I wish I could. At least I can tell you *have* a mind. To be honest, there are a couple of women in class I wonder about."

Megan laughed, too, amazed. He liked her. He thought she was bright. And she had let them all intimidate her.

"You're doing wonders for my confidence," she said.

His eyebrows went up. "Your confidence? Wait a minute. Didn't you just say you've opened a pre-school?"

She nodded.

"And you have children of your own?"

"Four. Between sixteen and four years old."

He shook his head. "How long has your husband been gone?"

"Since March."

"Confidence, Megan! You ought to be teaching a survival course."

She tried to laugh, although tears suddenly smarted in her eyes. "I haven't done that well. Just ask my kids."

"Listen. I work all day with people who cope through putting pills or alcohol into their mouths. And not one of them has had anything harder than that to deal with."

She looked at him. "But they must have. Or maybe they were younger or more vulnerable, somehow. Until now, I'd always been lucky, you know, always just . . . happy."

He took a drink and nodded. "You're right. I'm over-simplifying things. Chemical dependency can grab you a lot of different ways. But still . . . you've done all right, obviously."

Their cups were empty. "Thanks for the Coke," Megan said, "and the talking. I guess you could see how upset I was." Somewhere deep she felt the anger sill glowing, as though the embers could smolder forever.

"Just gave me an excuse," Alan said smoothly, taking both cups and dropping them in a garbage can. "Are you parked in the lot? I'll walk you to your car."

On the way, he asked about her children. She described them: pretty Becky and her need to be popular; Scott, who wouldn't meet her eyes and yet helped her more than anyone else; Elinor and her box of pencils and long white braid; and Heather, who jumped into everyone's lap and heart.

"They sound great. I'd like to meet them sometime."

"You would?"

She pulled her notebook closer, feeling uneasy. What did she know about him really?

"I know that must sound abrupt. But I really

would . . . sometime. I have a daughter who's in California with her mother. I miss her a lot."

"Oh." Megan thought again about the discussion in class. Was he the reverse of the norm? A father who sent child support but seldom saw his daughter?

"Besides," he said, as she unlocked the car, "I'm hoping we're going to be friends."

She looked at him, but darkness lay across his face. Both his hands were deep in his pockets. She took a deep breath. "I think I'd like that."

He nodded. "Goodnight, Megan."

She drove home, feeling the car drawn from one puddle of light to the next under the street lights, the neon signs, and the faraway, almost invisible stars.

KRISTIN

The first Friday evening in September, Kristin and Megan went together to the Relief Society opening social. Each carried two dozen brownies.

"These look wonderful," Nancy exulted, taking a peek. "Maybe we should start the buffet with dessert."

The two lined up with the other women before a banquet table loaded with salads, relish plates, and rolls. Since they were near the end of the line, they had not finished their dinners when the program began.

Kristin looked up from a fruit salad to see six women take their places on black stools on the stage. She looked from face to face. They look different, she thought. What is it? She searched her mind for types—not Bountiful, not the east side of Salt Lake exactly, though there was some of that. The University of Utah? Definitely. Brigham Young University in Provo? Maybe.

Kristin finished a carrot strip and pushed her plate aside. The lights dimmed, and the six women lifted black folders and began to read from the letters and journals of women in the early history of the church.

One was the third wife of a pioneer and spoke of learning to get along with the other wives, of missing her husband when he was away, and of the birth of her first child. She told how the first wife had blessed her before her confinement.

Kristin glanced around her. Polygamy wasn't usually discussed quite so openly. It came up, a little guiltily, in Sunday school class now and then. The faces around her looked attentive and discreet in the dimmed room.

Another woman represented in the reading was a doctor. Her sister wives made it possible for her to study in the east. Another was a woman whose husband refused to take another wife and who, she believed, never became a bishop because of that refusal.

Kristin listened closely. She couldn't tell if Megan's interest was as keen as her own, except that when one woman described losing her twins to diphtheria, she and Megan simultaneously reached for their purses to get tissues. Through the eyes of these women, Kristin watched Utah being born.

When the lights went on, Kristin looked around eagerly. People were fidgeting with their hair and clothes. Megan looked tired, but Kristin leaped up from her chair, as if she had spent the last hour flexing muscle. She pressed her way toward the readers, who were gathering up their scripts and stools.

"Thank you," she said to a thirtyish-looking woman with kinky sandy hair. "That was great."

The woman turned and smiled, then introduced herself. Before she knew it, Kristin was caught up in a conversation with her and two other women in the group. They seemed to know everything about things that were barely mentioned at church: plural marriage, women giving blessings to each other, women pursuing careers even in pioneer times.

"Why is it," Kristin blurted, "that your program makes me feel richer and poorer at the same time?"

A tall, blond woman laughed and put an arm around her shoulders. "Here, I'll give you my phone number and you give me yours. Call me for a reading list if you want to. I'll let you know the next time one of us reads a paper or there's a discussion group."

Kristin scribbled her name and telephone number and said goodby. Megan touched her shoulder as the women moved away. "Are you about ready to go?" Megan asked.

"Sure. Sorry if I'm slow. Just let me tell Nancy what a great program that was. Some people might not think so, but I'd like to encourage her to do something like that again."

Megan nodded and followed Kristin toward a cluster of women on the other side of the hall. As they approached, Kristin heard Nancy say, "I didn't think she'd changed much since — you know — but just *look*."

"Oh, I think so," Lisa answered. "She looks more like . . . well, tougher, more like . . . I guess she has to be."

"Photographs," Kristin said, raising her voice a little, hoping Megan hadn't heard.

"Didn't you see them?" Lisa asked quickly. "They're of the ward Christmas party. Bob just got around to developing them. This one of Megan is so attractive."

Kristin took the picture and held it so Megan could see, too. In it, Megan was talking to someone whose shoulder and ear blocked the right corner of the photo. Her eyes were alight, her face smiling, one finger poised under her chin. Megan reached for another photo, but Kristin looked longer at the first. It was Megan, all right. But she hadn't seen her make that gesture for a long time. It had once seemed so natural. Tough, they'd said. They meant more like me. Maybe she is, Kristin thought.

Kristin looked through the other snapshots quickly, then noticed that Megan was staring at one, almost transfixed. The others were busy ordering copies of their favorites.

"Megan?"

She looked up. "It's Richard."

There was a loud silence.

Kristin held out her hand. "Isn't that the one with Bill and George talking?"

Megan nodded. "He's in the background." She handed it over almost reluctantly.

Kristin expected to see Richard as a vague shape against a wall or a brooding figure slumped on a folding chair. But, looking, she was surprised she hadn't seen him before. He was actually in the center of the photograph, caught between Bill's and George's laughing profiles. And he wasn't alone. He wasn't brooding. He was talking with

Judy Gregory, a young mother who'd moved from the ward but still lived in Bountiful.

It was Richard's pose that held Kristin's attention and that had obviously held Megan's. Richard was smiling into Judy's eyes, his arm extended along the back of her chair. His arm wasn't around her exactly, but it looked chummy, nevertheless. Their knees almost touched. She's probably talking about that two-year-old of hers, Kristin thought. And, while Richard smiled into Judy's eyes, his vantage point seemed also to offer glances down her red holiday blouse, Kristin observed. Hopefully, Megan hadn't such a suspicious mind.

Kristin looked up. The group was watching her now, and she could feel Megan's tension. "Sorry," she said, handing over the photograph. "It was a terrific program, Nancy. Let's have something like that again."

"Glad you enjoyed it," Nancy replied. No one seconded Kristin's endorsement.

"Shall we leave, Megan?"

As they left the hall, Kristin looked back. The group had closed like a pond. The photograph of Richard flipped like a fish in Nancy's extended hand.

Kristin drove a silent Megan home. She stopped out front, under the boughs of a maple. "Would it be worth calling Judy?" she asked.

Kristin hoped Megan wouldn't leave the car yet. To her relief, Megan sat still and shook her head. "No." She cleared her throat. "I see Judy all the time. Richard's leaving doesn't have anything to do with her."

"I think you're right. I mean that snapshot is half a second out of a two-hour party . . . "

"Don't," Megan interrupted. "Tell me the truth, Kris. Didn't that picture surprise you? Is that the way you envision Richard? Was he . . . you know, a . . . " She reached for the right word.

"Was he always coming on to other women?" Kristin asked for her. "No, I never thought of Richard that way. He was a nice guy. Yes, Meg, it surprised me."

"It's just . . . a new way of looking at him, I suppose. I've wondered before if he could've left me for someone but only when I wanted desperately to believe he was alive anywhere and that he would come back. I hadn't considered it seriously. If he did, it would mean he's alive. But it would also mean," her voice cracked, "that he dumped it, dumped us, dumped everything . . . just for . . . "

She was sobbing. Kristin reached out and took her in her arms and let her cry, as if she were Bonny or Sheri. She hoped Nancy would not come home for a while.

"Why, Kris?" Megan kept asking once the sobs had subsided.

"That's the one with no answer."

"But we were happy. We were!" Megan straightened. She reached in her purse for tissues and patted her face dry. "Weren't we? Didn't you see it? Don't cry, Kris."

Kristin tried to laugh. She thought of the photograph of Megan, of the sweet expectation in her face like a good child's before Christmas. "Yes. You were happy. and you were good to him. Richard's leaving doesn't have anything to do with you, either!"

Megan shook her head. "It's not that easy. I should have seen it coming. There must have been some sign."

"Stop it!" Kristin said. "You can't afford to blame yourself. If Richard had a crush, he should have discussed it or handled it. If he was happy, he should have said so. What he did was inexcusable." Kristin realized that Megan was no longer listening and stopped.

"Kris," Megan said, "I just remembered. One night I came into our bedroom and Richard was on the phone."

Kristin waited.

"I didn't really hear anything, he just sounded hushed, intense. Actually, he'd hung up by the time I was really inside the room. I asked him who it was, and he said he could never get away from work, even at Christmas. Then he groaned and stretched out on the bed and shut his eyes. So I left him alone. Now, I wonder. But then, I don't know. I thought his tone was odd. Still, it was only a day or two before Christmas, and my head was full of a hundred other things."

In the pause that followed, the porch light on Megan's house went off, then on again. Megan chuckled. "Becky's signalling me. That's how I warn her to quit necking and come in after a date."

Kristin laughed, too. "And she probably says, 'But, Mom, we were only talking.' "

"How did you know?" Megan sighed and stretched her legs.

"You've been through so many theories, Meg," Kristin said. "Tomorrow you may wake up and think this one is absolutely bizarre."

"I know. But I don't think I will. In a way, this one's the most devastating. But you know what? There's a funny feeling of relief as if, finally, this is it. I've never felt this way before. Isn't that strange?"

"Maybe. If you're right, then Richard's not nearly as bright as I'd thought."

"Thanks for listening, Kris. Becky's tending for you tomorrow, isn't she?"

"Yes. Greg and I are going on a picnic. Let's do something afterward."

Kristin watched Megan walk to her door and thought about the four children inside — and recalled the photographs: Megan bright and happy and Richard listening to Judy and looking down her dress. She jammed her foot down on the accelerator, the tires leaped away from the curb with a squeal. But then she spotted Nancy's powder blue station wagon turning the corner. She lifted her foot, waved a careless hand, and demurely steered her Volkswagen toward home.

"You're early, aren't you?" Kristin asked as she opened the door for Becky.

"I jogged," Becky replied. "Mind if I get a drink?"

Kristin looked at the clock. She had her jeans, still on the hanger, in one hand a brush in the other. "Help yourself. You must jog fast. It's only eleven."

Becky drank deeply from one of the kids' plastic mugs. "Thanks. The thing is, Mom and Alan are playing detective again, so I decided to leave early."

"Well, the girls are next door swinging. You can turn on the television, if you want. Of course, not much is on Saturday morning. I guess that's why I'm going on this basic autumn picnic. Greg, my date, is on call at the clinic tonight."

Kristin nearly tripped over PC on her way back to the bathroom. "PC, for heaven's sake, go talk to Becky," she said sternly. PC trotted toward the back porch. Kristin hid a smile as she went to get ready. Like PC, she'd never felt completely easy with Becky. She had, in fact, been surprised when Becky agreed to babysit.

"Come on back, PC," Becky called airily and drifted into the living room. Kristin hurried into the bedroom to get dressed. When she came out, zipping her jeans, Becky was leaning beside the door like Bonny did. "How's the boy friend?" Kristin asked. Becky seemed more approachable — or was it vulnerable — than usual. Maybe she missed her mom, as well as her dad.

"Court's cute as ever. Hey, you really look great."

"For an old person?" Kristin egged. Becky laughed self-consciously.

"Well," Kristin continued, adopting a confidential tone, "Greg seems like a reasonably nice guy. He's a doctor who's just barely divorced. I wish I could have a long talk with his ex-wife and find out what I need to watch out for."

"You sound like Mom. She tenses up every time she sees a male, except maybe Scott."

"Or Alan?" Kristin suggested with as much curiosity as sympathy. Alan always seemed to be over there the evenings Kristin was free.

"Alan. Yeah. You know what? The bishop came by Sunday, the first time in ages. Mom was so uptight. I asked

her about it afterward and she said she's just so angry at
Dad right now that sometimes it carries over to other men
even if that's not fair."

"Mmmm," Kristin considered, looking into Becky's
young face. Her freckles showed today. "I'm not so sure it's
completely unfair. You can't help but feel that way after expe-
riencing something like what your Mom's been through."
Becky inspected a fingernail, and Kristin decided to lighten
up. "So your Mom hasn't noticed that Alan is male?"

"I mentioned it to her. She didn't even smile, just
sighed and said she tries to overlook it."

Kristin rolled her eyes and they both began laughing. "That's generous," Kristin cackled. "And how does Alan
like having his manhood overlooked?"

"I guess he can tolerate it," Becky giggled. "Anyway, Mom acts like she's alive again. She cleans the house
and runs that pre-school. Elinor and Heather have even quit
looking like orphans."

"Good for her. Hey, follow me into the bathroom.
You're fascinating company, but I've got to get ready."

Becky sat on the toilet lid. "Were you ever that
angry?"

"Are you kidding? I still burn sometimes." She put
on a fierce face before she picked up the brush again. "But
I'm afraid my Relief Society sisters caught most of my anger.
I should have taken it out on the priesthood, but they weren't
as accessible."

"Alan's a Mormon," Becky said.

"True. I finally asked your Mom about that. Usually I can tell, but with Alan I wasn't sure."

"Mom wasn't sure at first, either. She said that's because Alan's father is Jewish and his mother used to be Catholic. When he was fifteen, his parents got divorced, then he and his mother met the missionaries and joined the church and came to Utah."

"No wonder."

"What?"

"That I couldn't tell. No genetic secondary characteristics. I knew he was too relaxed to be *all* Mormon."

Becky smiled nervously. "He sure likes to talk. I don't think I've ever known a guy who liked to talk as much, at least not with a girl or a woman. Alan will even have these big conversations with Elinor."

"Not like your Dad, huh," Kristin said softly.

Becky sighed.

"Look," Kristin said, reaching for her eye shadow, "you're a kid. You're what? Sixteen? You shouldn't feel in the middle of your Mom's problems. Worry about your own love life."

"That's why I left early today. Alan fires questions at Mom, then she tries to remember. Sometimes I look over and she's crying without any sound. Had Dad been moody lately? Alan asks. Had there been unexplained absences? Did Mom talk to his boss? did she talk to his friends? Did the police search the foothills? Did they drag the creek? The whole thing gives me the creeps."

"I can see why. Well," Kristin held up three shades of lipstick, "what's your opinion? Lush Raspberry, Perfectly Pink, or First Blush?"

"Go with the raspberry. It brings out the mauve in your top. I love that print."

Kristin drew the lipstick over her mouth. They were both silent while she fluffed out her hair, brightened her cheeks, and touched up her eyelashes.

"Well?"

"Terrific. What's this guy's name again?"

"Greg. Dr. Greg Peterson. Nice ring to it, no?"

"Very nice. Sometimes I go around muttering Mrs. Courtney Kenney. It's dumb. Once in a while I get tired of him."

"Join the club," Kristin said lightly. "Don't take him seriously, Bec. You've got plenty of time for that."

Becky said nothing. Kristin guessed she'd heard it all before. "The girls ought to be home any minute. There's stuff for sundaes in the fridge. Bribe them with it about three when their blood sugar drops and they start fighting. Then think up something for them to do before they hyper out."

"Right."

"As long as you know where they are, feel free to talk on the phone."

When Bonny and Sheri burst into the house, they brought Kristin's date with them. Kristin looked at her beaming daughters. "Well, Greg, those chimps on your arms are actually my girls."

"This is Bonny and this is Sheri," he smiled as the girls beamed even brighter.

"Very good. And this is Becky Stevens and this is PC."

"For?"

"Prince Charming," Kristin said, distracted but not sure why.

"No," Sheri flounced. "For Peaches and Cream, Mom."

Kristin saw amusement in Greg's eyes and felt her color rise. "You be good kids for Becky. I'll see you before supper time."

That picnic remained in Kristin's mind as a careful minuet in the autumn woods. When one of them would move an inch closer with a word, a glance, a smile, a brush against the skin or clothing, the other would move back. Their afternoon was as precise as if they had practiced — so decorous and disciplined. When Greg brought her home she didn't ask him in more than half-heartedly, and he said he had to get home. She walked into the house feeling drained.

There was a full-scale performance just beginning in the living room.

"An audience!" Bonny squealed, swishing Kristin's blue winter cape around her. "I'm the wicked stepmother. Hurry and sit down."

Kristin did. She watched as Bonny pressed upon Sheri a poisoned apple. Becky narrated, then played the handsome prince, her hair gathered into a tight bun.

"Wonderful," Kristin applauded at the end. "Bravo!"

"We could do an encore," Sheri said hopefully.

Kristin laughed. "Give me a hug instead. I'll pay Becky, and then let's all walk her home."

"Okay. I wanted to see Elinor anyway," Bonny said.

Kristin was relieved that Alan wasn't there when

they all filed through the front door. "If I call out for pizza
do you have something we could drink?" she asked Megan.
"The last thing I want to do tonight is cook."

"Sure. And I'll fix a salad."

"Don't bother. I don't want you to cook, either."

"A salad isn't cooking," Megan said. "You kids scoot.
We'll call you when the pizza comes."

Kristin made the call, then watched as Megan moved
around the kitchen. "You're looking like a new person," she
said. "You've lost weight, haven't you?"

"I think so. I have a lot more energy. So much gets
done now and it feels great."

"Burning anger?"

Megan smiled. "Well, what am I supposed to do
with it now that I've finally dug it up?"

"Burning is a lot better than sitting on it," Kristin
said. Why *hadn't* Greg wanted to come in, she wondered
suddenly. Were the kids too much? But they'd been so cute
in that play. She sighed and tuned in to what Megan was
saying.

"The thing is, it finally sank in how I kept getting
put down. And by women who are just like me, really, right
down to the garment lines we can all see under our clothes.
I mean, we are sisters right to the skin, and beneath that.
Yet they keep shunning me like a leper. I know I'm exag-
gerating, but I can feel it. Am I that different?"

Megan whirled with toast for croutons in her hands.
"What arrogance! Don't they realize it? It's practically built
in. And the contempt. They don't even know it's there." She
threw the toast on the table. Her hands went up instantly,

then she brought them down in a shrug. "I was the same way, wasn't I."

"So was I," Kristin said. "Encased in an eggshell armor."

"Funny thing. After I got mad, I stopped feeling blue so often. But the anger still comes and goes. I sometimes wish I could control it better."

"It's doing wonders for you." Meg laughed, but loneliness had enveloped Kristin. She tried to shake it off. "Where did this comes from?" She touched a sparkling glass terrarium on the kitchen table.

Megan laughed again. "Alan brought it over. It's symbolic. He claims that's where I want to live. Right inside this carefully designed glass ball. Now that my world has shattered, all I want is a repair job, Alan says. 'You're free! You're free!' he tells me. He says I'm like an emancipated slave who wants to reconstruct the plantation."

"And do you?"

"Last week I wanted Richard back so I could tell him I love him and forgive him no matter what. If he's just still alive. This week I want him back so I can punch him out."

Kristin laughed now. "I guess I still want to glue the glass ball back together, myself. I have hope for it." She watched Megan whirl between the counter and the refrigerator. "You look like you're just running on nuclear fission."

"That's what it feels like. I'm going to see Richard's boss on Monday, and you know what? I can't wait. I want some answers."

Kristin said nothing. The way Megan's eyes snapped

was something she hadn't seen for a long time. In fact, today Megan looked like the Megan who hadn't been so friendly before. For a moment, Kristin found herself missing the sad Megan, her friend.

"Kris? How was the picnic?"

"It was fine. Not a thing wrong with it. But I'm pooped. And a little uptight. Do you know what I mean?"

"Let's do something after supper," Megan suggested. "At last, here comes the pizza." She followed Kristin to the living room, still talking. "You can leave your girls here. Becky's going out, but Scott will be around. Let's go for a run."

"Please. I've just been hiking. How about a swim?" She pulled her wallet out of her purse and paid the freckled young man who balanced a pizza box high on one hand.

———

Kristin did the backstroke lazily while Megan swam lap after lap, then started diving. Kristin put her hands on the bottom of the pool, stretched into a handstand, then returned to her slow swishing from end to end.

She heard loud voices and put her feet down on the bottom on the shallow end. A plump figure in a blue suit was waving at her from the diving board, where Megan stood talking.

"Hi, Nancy," Kristin called. "Hi, Lisa, Carol."

They took a long time, Kristin thought critically, to ease into the pool. But they did applaud Megan every time she dove. Kristin wondered whether or not Megan appreciated that. *She* wouldn't do it.

Kristin dove and swam underwater around the deep

end, surfacing only to breathe. She thought about dolphins. She thought about Greg. She thought about swimming with Greg, the two of them sleek as dolphins. Once she looked for the others. The trio was swimming slowly, back and forth across the mid-point between deep and shallow. She could hear their voices.

Kristin hoped no one would mind her keeping to herself. She didn't want to talk, and she silently thanked Megan for laughing and joking with them. Maybe Megan was feeling comfortable with them after all. Or trying hard. Kristin sighed and dove again.

When she and Megan finally got out, the trio followed them into the locker room. Lisa and Carol were comparing notes on whose husband had the most extracurricular activities on Saturday. Nancy, being Relief Society president, couldn't even list everything she had to do by Sunday morning. The three professed exhaustion, then happily comforted each other. Megan said nothing.

Kristin was sleepy and ready to go home. Like the others, she peeled away her suit, thinking how wonderful her dry clothes would feel. Even as a child, she'd loved the feel of clothing, suddenly soft and warm, on her water-weary body. She looked around. Standing there were the three women, nude, their backs to each other, their soaked suits on the floor. Kristin thought how much alike they all were, toweling, lifting one arm, then the other, rubbing flanks, thighs, calves, then feet. No one else turned her eyes from her own towel to notice the rhythm.

Still watching as the women dropped their towels and reached for their white garments, Kristin was entranced with the pattern. Later she tried to recall what they had been saying but couldn't. Only that their voices had been richly secure and that their complaints had reeked of that luxury.

Kristin was nearly dressed when she realized that Megan, on her other side, had stopped moving. "See you," Nancy said, her eyebrows up. "Right," Kristin said and smiled at them at they left.

Turning toward Megan, she saw the cause of Nancy's raised eyebrows. Megan was nude, her back turned toward the others. Her body had dried completely, Kristin noticed, and she was just beginning to shiver. Her gaze at the garments in her hand reminded Kristin suddenly of Sheri's horrified glare during the play when it had seemed she was peering into the heart of the poisoned apple her sister offered.

"Megan?"

Megan didn't reply or attempt to cover herself. Kristin shivered in the quiet locker room. The moment suddenly seemed odd, disjointed, as if she had skipped a page, or several, in a novel. What had she missed? Then Megan looked up at her, eyes stricken, and back at the garments in her hand.

"Meg."

Was there a muttered word or a sob as Megan shook her head? Kristin watched her take two stiff steps and drop her garments into the metal container that said PUSH. Then she silently put on the rest of her clothes.

Kristin sat down on the bench, face in her hands on her knees. She was dizzy and for a moment thought she'd be sick. Whose pain was this? Hers or Megan's? Finally, the air around her steadied. She looked at Megan, bent away from her to fasten her sandals. "Okay," said Megan, her face still averted.

Megan held out a hand, and Kristin took it and stood, squeezing as she fumbled with her bag. They walked together to the door.

As Kristin pushed open the locker room door, she touched Megan's shoulder in reassurance or warning. "It's going to be a cold winter," she said. When Megan looked at her, Kristin saw the fierce tears on her face.

13

MEGAN

Sometimes Megan almost believed she was superhuman, maybe in contrast to having felt subhuman for so long, but it seemed more than that. Increasingly, she woke up eager for whatever the day held.

I'm alive, she'd think when she saw apricot clouds through the curtains against a baby blue sky. Had the world always been so lovely? Everything seemed outlined with a fine dark line. Her children, familiar things in the neighborhood, everything stood out separate from the background. She saw what no one else seemed to see and spun through the days with an energy no one else seemed to have. Patterns emerged in people's words, in the flow of traffic. Everything swayed to a rhythm she heard through the soles of her feet. Somehow she had deciphered a code. What she read in the world now, she could not articulate or question, only pray it would last.

Despite these spells of euphoria, Megan had to admit that Kristin had been right about not wearing garments. Megan did feel chilly. More than that, when she recalled the slide of the soft, opaque fabric on her skin, or the pinch if she stretched too far, she felt guilty and exposed. Still, the texture of unaccustomed fabrics intrigued her. She had forgotten how different silk felt from flannel, how a skirt rippled over the legs. Her body seemed less shielded, less hidden. That bothered her sometimes, yet she had to confess she liked it and felt more herself. Shedding that insulation had tightened her connection to life.

She wondered whether anger still lay below her energy, her confidence. Whatever it was, it felt good to be able to decide what to do. About church, for instance. Kristin believed she must stay for all three meetings, even if nothing said there fit her life and even if something offended her. Megan had always felt similarly but not any more. If she thought sacrament meeting would give her a headache, she ducked out after Sunday school. Some weeks she stayed home and read or listened to music. Kristin could live on the edge of conflict if she wanted.

Sometimes Megan went to Alan's ward. His tolerance for people amazed her. One week at fast and testimony meeting the mother of a newly christened baby stood to bear testimony. The woman explained that she had spent most of the pregnancy on her back. She thanked the Relief Society for looking out for her six children, the oldest of whom was a girl who looked about eleven. The woman thanked the ward for fasting through her emergency

Caesarean section and for their prayers for the fragile baby. Now, the woman said, it was time to rejoice.

Megan saw the tears drip from her jaw on to the baby's blanket. There was a grayish cast to the mother's skin that made Megan's heart sink. Listening closely, she realized that Kristin had told her about this premature birth. Kristin had shaken her head. "Problems," she had said. "You wait and see."

But here was the woman, claiming her triumph. She confided that her doctor had told them not to have more children, yet the Lord had blessed them with two since then. Maybe one more spirit awaited them. Maybe a boy. By the time the woman sat down, her hands dripping from wiping tears from her chin, Megan was appalled but resigned to what would undoubtedly follow. Other testimonies were voiced, about miscarriages, infertility problems, determination to have children — the more the better — whatever the cost. In closing the meeting, the bishop praised the testimony bearers for their faith.

"Alan!" Megan burst out, even before they reached his car. "How will any woman in your ward use common sense again? This competition, it's . . . human sacrifice."

"Sure is," he said, making a beeline for his red Pinto. "Isn't that what religion is all about?"

"But," she sputtered, "what about those other children in that first woman's family? What about the baby? What about that poor woman? Why isn't her life worth as much as some poor little spirit's, who may just be imaginary anyway? It's a . . . fertility rally, you know that?"

"Get in the car, you heretic," he teased, shutting the door. He got in and took her hand, holding it flat on the seat where, Megan noticed with relief, no one outside the car was likely to notice. "I know, Meg. It hurts. But these are just people. What do you expect?"

"But how can you excuse them defaulting their decisions? You know, when bishops or husbands give bad advice in the name of the priesthood that hurts people."

"I know. I don't excuse that. It's just that . . . " He started the car, sighed, then looked back at her. "Half of the people in my drug and alcohol unit are Mormons."

"They are? Well, they're probably not good Mormons or they wouldn't be hooked on drugs and alcohol."

He shook a finger. "See how judgmental? They're all good people. At least most of them. And when Mormons start drinking either they're so guilty or so vengeful, it can be pretty damn hard to stop."

"I guess that makes sense." She took a deep breath, tried to calm down. Wasn't she the one who no longer got upset at church? Or so she told Kris. "Okay, I've composed myself. I try to strike a balance between your serenity and Kristin's fine sense of outrage."

"Are you insinuating that Kris and I are both unbalanced?" Alan asked. "That's okay. As long as we fill your needs."

"Oh, quit sounding like a therapist." She gave him a push. He let go of her hand and backed out of the parking place. The wheels spun, all connected to Alan's hands, and trees and sunset filled the windshield as they whirled into

the street. Megan felt happiness splash over her like the
short-lived sun.

The seven children who banged on the Gingerbread
House door each morning and the four who came in the
afternoon had become major characters in her life. Benjy,
Jason, Erin, Bucky. Each was an individual, not just the
child of someone in the neighborhood. Megan found herself
puzzling about their quirks after hours and repeating their
funny comments at the dinner table. She hired a neighbor's
mildly retarded daughter, Roxy, to come and help. Elinor
could supervise everything in the late afternoon, giving Megan
a much-needed break.

Now Megan rushed through housework while getting the children off to school and while grabbing a sand-
wich at noon. Really, that seemed enough time to spend on
housecleaning. The house had become scenery, nice but not
crucial to the plot.

Funny, but despite all the people who mattered to
her, Megan now saw herself in the central role. Before she
had doubled as stage manager who attended to all the details.
What's more, she felt that she'd been acting on the wrong
stage, and now she was Megan again — Megan at eighteen
before she'd married Richard — but tougher and wiser. When
she looked in the mirror, she recognized that eager, slightly
distracted face. Between eighteen and now, who had paused
here so often to scrutinize every pore, every hair, her eager-
to-please eyes wide open like a doll's?

But sometimes that new confidence dissolved so completely she wondered if she had made it up. Without it she

became gray and amorphous like a slug in a garden of but-
terflies. She set herself task after task, determined not to
collapse. She couldn't collapse now. She was on Richard's
trail.

Still, going to see Richard's boss was a problem,
since he only worked weekdays and so did she. Finally, she
kept Elinor out of school for the morning and asked Roxy's
mother if she would check on the girls every once in a while.
Then she drove to Salt Lake, pulled in the visitor's parking
lot near the Capitol, and walked briskly with shaky knees to
the office where Richard had worked.

"How are you, Mrs. Stevens?" she heard after a brief
wait.

"Fine, Mr. Anderson. Thank you for your time."

"You're welcome to it. I just hope I can be of some
help. Here, please sit down."

"I should have come sooner, I know, but . . . " She
felt herself fading a little, like Caspar, the friendly cartoon
ghost that a younger Becky had loved. She started again. "I
want to ask you some questions about Richard. As you may
know, I still haven't heard anything from him, and the police
haven't found anything, either."

Mr. Anderson shook his head sympathetically.

"Did you notice anything unusual about him those
last few weeks?"

"No, I can't say that I did. I thought about it at the
time, Mrs. Stevens, and that's why I can answer you so
promptly. He did seem sick that morning, but before that
he'd seemed fine. Of course, we'd recently finished the leg-

islative session, so everyone was exhausted, but the pressure was off."

"He did seem tired. And I thought he was quieter than usual."

"Oh? I don't remember that. He did yeoman's duty during the session, even though we had some graduate students here helping. Sometimes I think they take out people's time more than they save it, but Richard was very patient — humorous, really. You know how he could bring out that dry wit."

"Did he spend a lot of time with the graduate students?"

"I don't really know. You could ask some of the others about that. There were four students, if you want to talk with them. You know Jim and Sue and the other researchers, of course."

"Yes, I'll check with them, too. Do you have the names of the students?"

He shuffled through a file and pulled out a sheet of paper. "There you go. You can see that several live out of state."

"Yes, well, I'll write letters I suppose." Megan copied down the addresses, one in Arizona, one in Idaho, and two in the Salt Lake suburbs.

"Do you know if Richard had any close friends at work? Anyone he might confide in if something was wrong or if he was in trouble?" Her throat suddenly felt tight. She swallowed hard.

"No, Mrs. Stevens, I'm sorry but I don't. Richard

was pleasant to everyone, but I don't know if there was anyone like that."

They went over the morning he was last seen. Nothing new.

"Well," Megan said and put her pen and notebook
in her purse.

Mr. Anderson leaned forward. "May I ask, if you
don't mind, what do you think happened?"

"At first I thought Richard had been kidnapped or
something like that. Now I believe he's alive somewhere.
Beyond that, I just don't know. If anyone has any information at all, my children and I would appreciate the help."
She stood up.

"I understand." He seemed sincere, and opened the
door.

Megan walked into the hall. She almost expected
Richard to pass her, his shoulders straight under a tweed
coat. She could hear his light, confident walk. He'd always
looked right in these halls, the way some men look right in
a saddle.

She clutched the drinking fountain as she bent to
drink. Tears began dripping slowly into the pooling water.
Damn you, she thought, breathing deeply. His even voice,
his quick laugh, hovered everywhere. She decided to talk
with his co-workers another time or write them when she
wrote the graduate students. She pooled the icy water in the
stainless steel basin and dipped her fingertips in, then touched
them quickly to her eyelids. She had to get out.

She hated being there. She was Richard Stevens's
wife, and he had chosen to leave her, their four children,

and the seventeen years that comprised nearly half of her life. How must that appear to other people? Like it did to her. She walked out to the car and drove home shaking. She voluntarily gave the right of way to other cars. Even when it was her move, she felt sure she was somehow in the wrong.

Alan took one look at her that evening, gave her shoulders a quick squeeze, and turned his attention to the little girls.

"Where's Bec?" he asked Elinor, plopping down beside her on the couch.

"At Heidi's house doing homework, or so she says. Scott's at a scout meeting, thank heavens."

Alan winked at Megan, who shook her head. He let Elinor beat him at Chinese Checkers, balanced on a flat cushion between them, then played her again, coaching Heather to help him make his moves. This time he won. "Next time you can team up and both beat me," he teased.

Megan sent the girls off to bed.

"Okay, tell me," Alan said, when they were gone. She did, still feeling vague, disoriented. "I should have known," she said, "that it wouldn't do any good."

"Where are those names?" Alan asked. He looked them over, then took down the names of the other researchers. "So are you going to talk with these people?"

"I don't know." Why did he have to press her? "Alan, it was a creepy feeling there. I just wanted to get out."

"Why creepy? It reminded you of Richard?"

"No, it's more than that. When Richard was there, I felt like I belonged in a way, you know? People knew me.

Richard helped to define me. I was Richard's wife. Today I felt like a ghost."

She could use one of those long, brown accepting looks right now, but instead his eyebrows were quirked, his voice intent. "Well. How *do* you think of yourself?"

"I've just been thinking Megan Stevens lately. You mean as far as Richard is concerned?"

"Either. He left you without status, right? Maybe without identity, too. In my book, that's a crime. Do you think of yourself as married or as single?"

"Neither," Megan answered and found herself unable to meet his eyes. She took a deep breath and tried to be matter-of-fact. "I am married, but he's gone. I'm not single, but I might as well be. I'm not a widow as far as I know, and people treat me like I'm divorced, but I haven't been. No wonder I feel like a ghost."

"So what can you do? I see only one thing."

"So do I."

She met his eyes, then wondered why he was looking at her in that way, his eyes completely serious, his humor utterly gone. Suddenly she was uncomfortable. "What were you going to say?" she asked nervously.

"Maybe the same as you."

There was a pause. Megan shrugged and tried a laugh to break the tension. "I was just going to say what I always say. All I can do is try to find him."

Something crossed Alan's face, but Megan couldn't say what. Curiosity opened her cloud a little. "Alan, what were you going to say? It wasn't that, was it."

"No." He stretched his long arms over his head and sighed. "I was just thinking about you clarifying your status."

"Oh." The moment lingered. "How?" she asked finally.

Unexpectedly he straightened. "Megan, you could divorce him. Simple grounds: abandonment."

Megan looked at Alan but didn't say a word. Eventually she stood and went into the kitchen. She watched abstractly as her hands took frozen lime and lemonade our of the freezer, turned on the cold water tap, then ran the cans under the can opener. Why haven't I considered that? she thought. He did leave me, didn't he. Isn't it my move now?

When she put the tall, cold glasses on a tray, she found her hands were trembling. She set the tray on the hearth in the living room. Alan was stretched out on the carpet, his head on a pillow. But at the tinkling of glass, he sat up. They each took a glass and drank. He looked at her. She looked at him, then away. "It's all right, Meg," he said. "I'm not lobbying."

"You're such a good friend," she said. "I just don't want anything to . . . " Her throat closed. She really hadn't thought it possible to lose anything more. But of course it was, she realized now. Alan set his glass down, then propped himself closer to her. He reached out one long hand and began rubbing her shoulders and back. "You're all tied up. Relax."

She was surprised. He seldom touched her, but his hand was warm and unhurried, and after a minute she relaxed, sipping at her drink silently. Comfort crept over her, so lovely, so longed-for, she was afraid she would weep.

Just then the door slammed open, hitting the opposite wall, and Scott rushed in. "It's raining like mad," he began, then stopped, staring at them. His words hung like the gust of wet air that came in with him. Alan didn't move, but as Scott gulped, shut the door, and walked quickly down the hall, Megan felt her neck and shoulders prickle and begin to itch.

SCOTT

If there was one thing Scott couldn't stand, it was a fumbler. When he thought of his dad he remembered his hands, not large, fine-boned really, but quick, tense, sure. He remembered his dad in the workshop, edging a piece of plywood toward the saw. He remembered him always winning knot-tying contests. Scott liked to think that his own hands were just like that, quick and sure. Two motions to zip a coat. Even loading a dishwasher was like putting together a puzzle if you thought about it.

This guy, Alan, Scott thought. He could spend fifteen minutes breaking and buttering a piece of bread that Scott could slick smooth in two seconds. Meanwhile he would talk, his hands moving, until the broken bread somehow became part of the conversation. Maybe stuff like that was charming to women. At least, Mom and Elinor and Heather seemed to love it. But he couldn't tell about Becky. She was usually off in a daze, probably over that guy Court.

Now Court, he could fumble a little more. Scott had heard Court was as smooth with girls as he was with a basketball. Scott had gone to the last practice with his friend Eddy, who was a freshman, which is what Scott would be next year.

"Hey, Eddy, who's your friend?" one of the guys had called out.

"Scott. Scott Stevens."

He'd seen Court look up, give him a measuring look, then a sideways wave that said hi, you're okay, in a second that Scott both appreciated and resented. Maybe he ought to tell Becky that Court was too cool for her. But he knew she wouldn't listen. If Dad were here, he'd tell Becky. Mom would be paying more attention, and Alan wouldn't be hanging around. At least Alan brought steaks or a huge bunch of black grapes or even a dozen chocolate doughnuts when he came. Luxuries. Maybe bribes. Not that Scott disliked Alan, but he'd just as soon see him a lot less.

At least his mother hadn't given Alan anything. She hadn't lost her head. Yet. Still, how cool if Alan saw him wearing his dad's cufflinks some Sunday (although he knew he'd first have to come up with a shirt with French cuffs). Dad had probably intended to leave him those cufflinks. But, "when you're eighteen," his mother had said, binding him to her. Forget that.

The night he walked in on Alan rubbing his Mom's back, he went straight to his room and started a letter.

Dear Dad,

Maybe this is dumb, writing to you when I don't know where you are. But you told me once about this link between us, and I guess that's what I'm counting on. I know you must have left for a real important reason. But things are getting a little out of control here. Although I've done my best to help out. We're not starving or anything, but everything's changing. If you could come home, I know the two of us could get things squared away, and then maybe this time you'd take me with you. I'm older now. I know you'll say Mom needs me, but I think she'll soon be doing okay on her own. That's the thing. Things have changed and if you had to leave because of the way things were, maybe now you could come back? If you see what I mean. Love from your son, Scott.

He took the letter, inserted it in an envelope, and wrote his father's name on the outside. Quietly, he looked out the back door. The rain had stopped. The air was soft and damp. He let himself out the back door, carrying the letter and a box of kitchen matches. Beside the door of what his mother now called Gingerbread House, he knelt, placing the letter on the sidewalk. He moved the letter to the dry spot by the door. He lit it and sat on his haunches, watching the smoke and ashes rise in the misty night.

"Scott?"

He jumped so hard he had to put a hand flat to catch his balance. November's mix of yellowed grass and mud squished under his fingers.

"I'm sorry." Now Becky was stooping beside him. "What are you doing? Hey, you're . . . burning something."

"Just a note," Scott said. "I didn't want anybody to read it."

Becky was quiet for a minute. Scott thought about getting up and going in, but something held him there with her in the dark driveway.

"Do you have any more matches?" Becky said after the silence had stretched until it fit comfortably between them.

"Yes." He shook them out on the sidewalk. "How come?"

She said nothing, just lifted her face to the breeze. He felt suddenly that they were children again, joined in some small mischief out of sight of their parents. They'd never told on each other. It was a pact.

"You look different," he said suddenly. Was it wind and rain that left her face so pale?

She smiled a little. "No makeup. I've been crying. I must look awful."

"Oh." Scott was afraid that now the spell had been broken. He'd better go in. But Becky reached inside her jacket and pulled out her pale blue scarf. She held it to her face for a minute, then lay it in a long streamer along the sidewalk. She picked up a match, struck it on the concrete as deftly as if she were still ten, and lit the scarf. Scott watched, astonished. The scarf smoldered and went out. Patiently, she relit it in six, seven places. It burned slowly, shriveling to ash then dust, leaving a chemical odor.

She didn't look at him, but said, "Court gave me that."

"That's what I thought."

She sighed. "We broke up. I hope."

Don't cry, Scott thought. But she laughed a little instead. "I wish you wouldn't grow up," Becky said softly.

"What?" He thought he'd heard her but wasn't sure.

"Nothing. Remember when we were little?"

"Yeah."

The silence squatted between them. They were both shivering, but neither made a move toward the back door. "You know what I burned?" Scott asked, surprising himself. "A letter to Dad. Dumb, huh."

"A letter from you?"

"Yeah. A note. Just telling him what's going on."

"You didn't ask him to come back?"

"Yeah, but then I burned it."

After a minute, Becky said, "Which way was the wind blowing? South? East? Let's say that . . . if we can figure that out, we'll know where he is."

Scott grinned. "You know what, Bec? Maybe neither of us should grow up."

Then they both heard voices and laughter, Megan's and Alan's, just before the back door opened and a rectangle of light flipped into the driveway.

"Sometimes I wonder if people really do," Becky said, "you know, if things ever really change."

Scott stood, gave her a hand up, and together they went inside.

15

MEGAN

Once in Salt Lake, the first thing they did was to drop off the kids at the Crossroads Mall, reviewing instructions about when and where to meet. Then Alan drove into the concrete maze of the ZCMI parking plaza, trailing a blue sports car through the slow turns to the top.

It was in the toy store that Megan realized that she would never finish shopping if Alan came along. She should have sent him with the children, so he could debate endlessly over one thing or another. She watched him dream over the games, frowning on those that ran on batteries, intrigued by the puzzles that promised insanity. Megan guessed that not even Scott would get those together again, let alone Alan.

Still, she took note of the tangle of nuts and bolts at which Alan gazed the longest. She could come back and buy it for him—a light, inexpensive, but thoughtful gift. In the end, Scott could solve it for him, and that would delight them both. Finally he joined her where she waited in line.

"Listen," she said, "most of my shopping is pretty pragmatic, once I've paid for this doll house furniture. Do you want to meet me in an hour after I've got the boring stuff done?"

He shrugged. "Okay. I'll meet you in front of the bank, there above the south escalators. I need to pick up a little cash for the weekend. Or I'll need to by the time I finish looking around."

He grinned as if the shopping expedition were simply a lark, when Megan could feel the pressure of only nine days until Christmas weighing heavily on her head and shoulders. "Hey, I've got a task for you if you want it: pencils for Elinor." His eyes gleamed—a challenge. "Good!" Megan said with relief. She hurried toward the nearest department store, mentally counting her dollars.

When she found Alan an hour later, he wasn't exactly where he'd said he'd be. He was standing outside Fred's restaurant on the bottom floor, leaning against the wall. One long hand held a chocolate malt.

He offered her a spoonful, but she shook her head. "When did you start eating ice cream? Every time *we* indulge, you accuse us of all the faults in Mormon culture."

He shrugged. "It's a Christmas tradition. One chocolate malt every year keeps away evil spirits. So how's the shopping?"

"Nearly done. I still have to find a long-sleeved blouse for Elinor. Want to help?"

He looked past her for a minute. "This is going to take me a while. If I eat it too fast, my sinuses ache."

"Unhealthy stuff, huh?" she teased.

"Don't you want to get some? Blueberry, maybe?"

"No, thanks. We're meeting the kids pretty soon for dinner, remember?"

"Oh, yeah." He stirred the malt thoughtfully. "Want to see the pencils I found?"

"Later, okay?"

"Okay. Well, why don't you finish up, then meet me back here."

Megan felt impatience rattle through her like a sudden gust. For a second she wanted to shake him. "Oh, all right. Can I leave these packages with you?"

She stacked the large sacks rustling at his feet, then walked briskly toward the escalator, stepping on behind a young woman in a blue business suit. Her long hair was precisely turned under. Maybe she's an attorney, Megan guessed, then noticed the run-down heels on her shoes. Maybe she's just starting out, she amended.

When the escalator lifted Megan above the opposite staircase, she caught a glimpse of a prone figure sprawled on the stairs — an old woman, she saw in alarm. A filmy red bandanna was tied in a triangle over the gray head, a short coat covered the top half of her cotton dress. A plastic shopping bag lay beside her. Megan saw the young woman ahead of her looking, too, as she stepped off the escalator and hurried to the top of the stairs.

"Is she all right?" Megan asked, joining her.

"I can see her breathing. It looks like she's asleep."

Now Megan could see that the woman's face rested on a book several steps above her body. Watching her nervously, looking for signs of life but careful not to disturb her—and afraid she was already so sick or dead she couldn't be disturbed—Megan saw the woman's shoulders shudder. The deep breath was held for a full minute before it exited. Megan wondered if sleeping on a staircase wasn't impossibly uncomfortable after all. The woman beside her met her eyes and smiled, as if she had the same thought.

Megan looked down a floor and saw Alan watching. He waved. "I guess she's okay," Megan said. She and the younger woman shrugged at each other and left.

By the time she met Alan the second time, the old woman was gone. While Megan had waited in line at the toy store again, with the nuts and bolts puzzle in her hand, she'd realized why Alan had bought that malt. Now she marched up to him and confronted him over the heap of shopping bags.

"Admit it," she accused, smudging a bit of ice cream from his cheek with her index finger. "You got that malt so you could watch over that old woman. Right?"

He smiled, then reached out and hugged her. "Says who? No wonder I had to give you an A in class. Always figuring things out."

"Admit it!" she insisted. "Don't pull rank on me." Her face grazed his coat, and she stepped back. "What happened to her anyway?"

"Oh, about five minutes before you came back she woke up. Perfect timing."

"So she was okay."

"Yes. She's a bag lady. Malls are warmer places to sleep than bus stops, I suppose."

Megan shivered. "I guess it wouldn't have been a good idea to call the police."

"What for? I wouldn't call ZCMI Security either. They'd just wake her up and tell her to move on — maybe not too gently."

"But, meanwhile, someone had to look out for her, right?"

"Did you see her bag lying there like that?" He wound his plaid muffler around his neck. "If someone swiped it, she'd lose all she owns. Except her Bible. She rested her face on that. Did you notice?"

They walked back to the parking plaza where the winter wind hit them in a freezing assault. She stepped on a small patch of ice and slid a few inches. "Come on," Alan said, tucking her hand in his pocket with his, like a bird in a nest. "When she got up," he added, "the Bible cover left a pattern on her cheek."

It seemed they would never get out of the crowded parking plaza, but soon they were holding up right lane traffic on First South as the children piled into the car, crackling with paper bags. Their bodies collided lightly as they found seats and argued over foot and package space. Elinor and Heather each had a silver helium balloon. Megan wasn't sure what those had to do with Christmas shopping, but she stuffed them on to her lap to get them out of Becky's and Scott's faces. She agreed that the balloons need not stay in the car while the family ate.

The clatter enclosed Megan and carried her into the

restaurant. There the children insisted on the table closest to the big stone fireplace, piling their coats high on an adjacent table until a fabric wall gave them a sense of privacy. And enclosed in the heat, Megan decided, shedding the V-neck sweater that matched her turtleneck.

While the pizza baked, Megan took the younger two girls to the restrooms. Alan had tied a balloon to each one's wrist, and Megan smiled to see the silver spheres gleaming above the closed stalls like friendly spirits.

As they ate, the children compared notes on the gifts they'd selected and those they'd considered and left behind. Scott teased Heather about Santa Claus, while Elinor remained smugly silent. They seemed not to need Megan to direct the conversation around sore points or to settle arguments. They included one another almost triumphantly and let Megan and Alan listen.

Alan lounged on a narrow stool attached to the table, his long legs emerging on Megan's side, ankles crossed. She watched the fire's light and shadow cross his face like thought. When he'd catch her eye, she'd smile. But behind her smile she wondered. It was as if he had nothing in the world to do but listen to this childish pandemonium as long as it lasted. He didn't seem to be eating much, spacing his bites of pizza between long sips of a tall 7-Up, but then Alan seldom ate much.

Becky's hair shone in the firelight, but she looked pale. Lately her makeup and curls had been replaced by a scrubbed face and smoothly brushed hair. Her light heart and demanding self-confidence seemed subdued. Megan was relieved and worried at this new aspect of her firstborn. But tonight even Becky's seriousness gave way to the evening's festivity. Becky never mentioned Court any more, but she seemed as busy as ever. Megan had expected Becky to be tense about Christmas. Surely she would be disgraced before her friends by an inadequate showing on Christmas morning, but Becky had said little about presents. Instead she'd plotted with Megan about gifts for the others. She'd been so unselfish that when Megan saw her sigh over a blue sweater in the mall, she had doubled back to overlook the price tag and buy it. Suddenly Megan had felt Christmas. Now every time she looked at Becky, she felt the glow return.

Scott was talkative tonight, his hands moving as fast as his words as he described to Alan the elaborate train set in the mall's lobby. Elinor stared into the fire more than she talked and chewed what surely must be her third piece of pizza. Her eyes were soft and dreamy, and tendrils of hair spiraled around her flushed face like a halo. Heather looped her arm firmly through Alan's while she ate, tipping to the left when she clenched both small hands on her glass of milk.

Megan knew she had no guarantee that Christmas itself would be so pleasant. Maybe it would be awful. But she relaxed into the evening's coziness like a kitten squirming into a heap of sleeping siblings, warm as Alan's brown glance that fell now on her face. Like her children, she managed not to picture Richard's pale face peering at them through some black window.

That night when Megan fell asleep in her queen size bed, she was thinking that surely Richard would call on Christmas. Or write a card. She wanted to call Elinor in to

help her warm the bed, but she was too weary and Elinor
was probably asleep.

Sometime in the night Megan awoke as suddenly as
if a voice had called her. She sat up. There was only the
hum of the refrigerator down the unlighted hall. She curled
into a ball, chilly, aware that her bed felt as stony and cold
as a flight of stairs.

ALAN

Alan left Megan's house early with the honest excuse he had to go to the grocery store before going home. He had picked up pork chops (Scott's favorite) and cookies on the way over, but he now needed the nitty-gritty of life. Toothpaste, peanut butter, vitamin C supplement to withstand January, and 7-Up for the ulcer that had healed without giving him much peace.

He walked the aisles of the grocery store feeling melancholy and suspended. Once he snapped to staring at a box of chocolate pretzel breakfast cereal. Finally he recalled Heather telling him about it before dinner. Megan wouldn't buy it, and Heather obviously hoped he would add it to the surprises that accompanied his visits. He read through the list of ingredients printed on the side of the box, shuddered, and set it back on the shelf.

He sighed, looking at his cart, still almost empty.
What did he need, anyway? Nothing. It just seemed that he
was always out of everything. He still seemed to spend so
much time thinking of food, maybe because some days his
stomach made him regret most of what he ate.

He would walk down every aisle and pay attention.
The folded paper in his pocket crackled slightly as he walked.
He and Megan had listed everyone who might know something about Richard: the other researchers, the graduate
students, two or three friends in the ward. Like most men
Alan knew, Richard called a lot of people friends, but they
were professional or church friends, not personal friends.

Megan had kept the list for weeks without calling
anyone on it. She had urged Alan to take it, and he had.
But he would resist doing anything without her, even though
his hand ached to pick up the telephone. He wanted to interview one person after another, driving hard for the secret
answer that would solve this mystery once and for all. He
could toss the solution in Megan's lap and say, "There you
go. Now you can marry me."

And then what?

Oddly, he didn't worry about Richard coming back.
Perhaps he should. Megan must be hard to forget. Certainly she had been memorable sitting in his class, quiet but
alert to every nuance. She'd reminded him of his clients
coming out of detox, painfully like new wet pots, as impressionable as the riverbank from which the clay came. Megan
wasn't recovering from a chemical dependency like his clients, but at first she intrigued and moved him in the same
way. The sheer pleasure of being in her company came later.

He wanted Richard *more* gone, not less. He wanted Richard's image erased from the inside of Megan's eyelids. He wanted her free from the inside out. But he would not make the same mistake he'd made years before.

He picked up Ivory Liquid, toilet paper, Kleenex, soap, and SOS pads. Rounding the corner, he added cheese, yogurt, pocket bread, then moved on for aspirin, Rolaids, and razor blades. He headed for the nearest checkout stand.

The girl checking groceries was, Alan guessed, no more than eighteen. She was pregnant. He looked at her hands and saw that she wore no rings. She was stout with reddish hair, so only her age and condition reminded him of Sunny when she came to the D&A unit soon after he became a counselor. Sunny had checked into that unit like destiny, an elfin, long-haired, pregnant eighteen-year-old who had come off pills in a hurry to protect her baby. She'd had to learn how to live without a buffer.

Alan, in his early twenties, was in some ways younger than Sunny, he thought now, although they'd both considered him much older. And Alan, learning to counsel, *had* helped. Naturally, they'd fallen in love. She'd battled her addiction, he'd helped, they'd married, she'd had Jani, and had fought the addiction some more. He'd helped. Finally when she won her independence from drugs, she had to free herself of Alan, too. They both accepted the end of their marriage as part of her emancipation, but it had hurt like hell. She had moved to California and taken Jani with her, and Jani had always belonged to them both.

She still does, Alan thought grimly, remembering

how her glossy hair fell around the pert face so like her mother's.

"There you go," the red-haired girl said, popping her gum. He picked up the sack, smiled at her, and carried the bag to his car.

No, Alan thought, pulling out of the parking lot. Megan had to fight her own war. He'd overpowered love once by running an exchange on need, sacrifice, and debt. A hundred things could happen to pull Megan away from him, but they'd be different things this time. Megan was coming into her own. He would give her no reason to need to outgrow him.

Instead of turning toward home, he took the road to the canyon. He needed sky and stars over a peaceful valley, maybe a walk if the air wasn't too frigid. He might be lucky and trip over Richard's bones.

He stopped the car by a small overlook and stepped outside. The night was crystalline, the stars like glass orbs in the black sky. Alan shoved his hands deep into his pockets. He blew a huge puff of breath into the air as he walked. The snow was soft along the road, just a few dry inches like powdered soap. He had no intention of tackling the drifts off to the side.

Twenty feet from the car, he realized that another car was parked just out of sight behind a stand of firs. He stopped, debating whether to turn back so soon or try to pass it inconspicuously. Probably a couple necking, he thought. Then he heard a word or a snort and looked again. He saw someone — a man outside the car, lifting up the hood. It looked like car trouble. Alan started toward him.

"Can I help?"

The man looked up, paused, then waved. "I could use a jump. I'm afraid the battery's dead."

"Just a minute." Alan jogged back to his car, but not before seeing a second figure huddled in the front seat. A marital summit meeting, he supposed. There was something about the man that suggested marriage. He wasn't a kid and seemed only mildly embarrassed.

Alan drove his car nose to nose with the other and, blowing steam, tried to make his chilling fingers attach the jumper cables properly. But the man shook his head and rearranged the clamps. "Okay," he called out. Alan started his car, then jumped out to undo the cables. He looked up from the crisscross between the engines into Becky Stevens's face through the windshield.

They stared at each other for a minute. Then Alan unhooked the cables and slammed down the hood on his car. When the man got out to do the same, he walked to Becky's window. She rolled it down.

"Do you want me to take you home?"

She shook her head and rolled the window up again.

The man was approaching now. "I appreciate your help."

Alan nodded. "I was just saying hello to Becky. I didn't realize she was here. She's a friend of mine."

"Is that right?"

There was a pause. The man blew on his fingers, then shook them. "Lovely girl, isn't she?"

Alan looked at him. "I'm Alan Goldmun," he said finally.

"Happy to meet you. I'm Boyd Leavitt. Becky's seminary teacher. She came to me after a seminary activity and asked to talk. She was upset, so we went for a little drive."

Alan felt Becky's door open against his leg and stepped aside.

"Alan," she said sweetly, "maybe you could give me a ride home. I hate to keep Brother Leavitt any later."

"Fine," Alan said, taking her arm. "Here, slide in this way."

Becky was quiet until they were out of the canyon. Alan wondered what she was thinking — or scheming. He wondered what she would tell Megan or whether she would leave it to him. When they saw the city's street lights, he said, "What did the seminary do tonight?"

"Do? What do you mean?"

"I thought maybe there was some activity."

"No, I don't think so."

There was a pause, then she looked at him sharply. She giggled. "Is that what Brother Leavitt told you? As far as I know, I was his only activity."

Alan looked at her, braking gently.

"Wait, I didn't mean it to sound that way. I mean, we were talking. He was teaching me. We pray and talk together, see? It's not like it was with Court. Brother Leavitt's more mature — like a father, only like a man, too."

"You don't see Court any more, do you?"

She shook her head. "No, it was just a physical attraction. I know that now. Brother Leavitt helped me see that."

"Mmmm," Alan said, trying to follow.

"Do you notice a difference in me, Alan? I mean, I

don't spend all my time on my hair and my nails. I'm not so vain anymore. Most of my friends have all but dropped me now that I don't wear any makeup and I'm not so silly. Doesn't it show?"

He nodded and smiled. "It shows, Becky. Your mother and I have wondered about the change. But, you know, you're not around much more than you used to be. At least you're often gone in the evenings."

She smiled.

"How old are you?" he asked suddenly.

"Almost sixteen-and-a-half. Why?"

"Just wondered."

"I seem older, don't I? I've grown up, Alan. A lot has happened to me lately, and I'm much more mature now." She sighed, and Alan bit back a smile. "With Court, I think I was just pretending to be young." A long breath, then: "Brother Boyd lets me know I'm a woman." Her tongue lingered over the name.

Alan pulled into the dark high school parking lot and turned off the lights but kept the heater running. They'd both been chilled enough for one night. "Becky, just what is your relationship with Boyd Leavitt?"

Becky looked out the window. "He's my seminary teacher."

"And?"

"A friend. My best friend."

"What about that girl—Heidi, wasn't it?"

"I still like her a lot. But lately we just can't talk."

"I see. Bec, everyone needs someone to try ideas out

on. Someone to trust. It doesn't matter how mature you are, you need that. Try me, okay?"

"I can't."

"Why not?"

"Because. You'll tell Mom."

He took a breath. "What if I don't?"

"Is that a promise?"

"It's a promise." His stomach throbbed, the same stab as when he picked up his fork to eat something spicy. He slid an arm along the back of the seat and turned toward her, half-encircling her without touching. "So, what's going on?"

"Nothing bad. As I said, he sees me as a woman, Alan, not a girl. Mary had the baby Jesus when she was my age."

"And Juliet married Romeo," Alan interrupted. "I know, I know. But you're still just sixteen."

"Well, I'm learning, too."

"Learning what?"

She paused. "The way they live," she said so softly he had to hold his breath to hear.

"The way who live?"

"The Leavitts. It's beautiful, Alan. It's awfully hard, but it's beautiful."

"So he's married."

She smiled, dimpled. "Oh, yes."

"Then what is his interest in you?"

Becky sighed. "Did you ever read Section 132 of the Doctrine and Covenants? Not everyone can live that way. Only the few."

Alan thought. The section sounded familiar, but he couldn't for the life of him remember what it said or what it had to do with Becky and her seminary teacher. "Do you like him, Becky? I mean love him?"

Becky's face went soft, and she looked him in the eyes. "I worship him, Alan," she said, her voice as sweet and clear as the stars. "Almost, I do. How can I tell you? Did you see his hands? When Court touched me it was exciting, but not holy. Not like this."

Alan watched her hold her hands before her, palms down. He knew she was not seeing her own shapely, small hands that trembled with cold or emotion.

He wanted to know more about how and how much Leavitt had touched her, but she had unfurled her love like a smooth, white cloth. He couldn't wipe his hands on it. He cleared his throat.

"Don't tell me you've fallen for that 'laying on of hands' line," he kidded, brushing back a strand of her hair casually. "That's as old as the hills and twice as dusty."

She wrinkled her nose at him, but the dreaminess didn't leave her eyes. She rubbed her palms briskly, then tucked them inside her coat. "There's no comparison between a kid like Court and a worthy priesthood holder like Boyd Leavitt."

"You've kissed him?" Alan asked. There was a silence. She didn't look at him, although she lifted her chin. "It's serious, Alan. Very serious."

Alan started the car. "What do you call him when you're with him?"

"Brother Boyd, like the others."

"The other students?"

"No. Come on, take me home, and remember: you can't tell Mom."

"Okay. But you promise me one thing, too."

"What?"

"That you'll talk to me before doing anything . . . major."

A pause.

"A promise for a promise," he prodded.

"Okay."

When she ran into the house, the lilt of her voice lingered in the car. Alan thought he had never seen anyone, not even Sunny, so young and vulnerable. He drove home with the heater blowing full blast, but he was still as cold as the dark valley.

He sighed. Lord, he'd done it again! Damn his empathy.

Food never added a pound to his bones, yet he understood the seduction of doughnuts and whipped cream to one whose heart was already encased in fat. He could get high on desert red rock or music or sunsets over the Great Salt Lake. Yet he *knew* in his marrow that ache for bliss, or security, that drove his drinkers and junkies into the arms of their demons.

Now his stomach was gurgling like a washing machine, and his arms and legs felt encased in lead. He burped and tasted acid. Empathy could weigh as heavy as the world. He knew how Scott felt, for example, how he relished a man's presence in the house and yet rejected Alan. Sometimes he wept inwardly for Megan; yet Kristin had hinted, once when she dropped by, that he was likely to hurt her. Now Becky. She sat like a stone in his gut.

When would he learn to stop taking in strays?

He chuckled. He'd had a roommate in college — Gary — who'd said that all the time. Quit taking in strays! There was the half-dead bird who crashed into the dorm window one morning and later all the cats that mewed around the doorstep every night. Finally Alan had freed himself of the most demanding entity in his life. He got a new roommate.

Alan, you're simpatico, Guillermo had told him, patting his shoulder one night when Alan wept with him after Gil's wife left him and took their children back to Mexico. Simpatico, you should have become a priest.

Section 132, Alan reminded himself, heading up his sidewalk. Unlocking the door, he realized that the section was famous — that's why it sounded so familiar. It contained the revelation on eternal marriage, first practiced as polygamy. Alan let his shoulder sag against the door. Why hadn't he realized that immediately so he could confront Becky? He knew there were polygamists in Bountiful, everywhere in Utah, but they blended in with everyone else. Suddenly everything Becky had told him made sense.

Then he remembered he'd promised not to tell Megan. Lord, now what? He would have a hot bath and a tall 7-Up. But he wondered if he would sleep.

MEGAN

Searching for Richard, Megan raised his ghost. Now that she had begun calling people in earnest, asking questions about Richard, and taking notes, she felt him lurking by the telephone. His enigmatic presence slid along the walls and trailed her from the kitchen into Gingerbread House. For the first time in months, she remembered the yellow, art-plastered room as the workshop it had been. The hammer, the sander, the roller pan that had become hers through use, once again sported Richard's fingerprints.

She kept calling people. She called Sue and Jim, the other researchers who had worked with Richard. She called Lloyd Patterson, his home teaching partner, and a couple of other men in the ward. Her lunch breaks and evenings were linked by these conversations. In between calls she wondered. Once again, the old arguments, theories, excuses and scenarios of reconciliation rang in her brain. Wasn't this natural to sense Richard lurking in corners again or trying to read her thoughts through the back of her head? He spoke sudden, meaningless phrases into her quiet moments; he breathed along her cheek.

Every tidbit of information became valuable, as if she were gold-panning for nuggets. Nuggets of *what* didn't matter so much, for she didn't know what she sought. Kristin had confided her last look at Richard — in the aisle at the grocery store. Lloyd had said Richard had seemed quieter than usual, more detached, the last time they went home teaching. He hadn't thought anything of it at the time. Sister Pugh, an eccentric, rich old lady in the ward, stopped her by the drinking fountain after Relief Society one Sunday to say she'd heard that Richard was preaching peace in Guatemala. Her grandson, on a mission there, had seen an Anglo who looked just like him.

"But when did your grandson ever see Richard before?"

"I just told you! He saw him one day in church and another day on the highway. He caught his eye, my dear, because he was with a stunning blond."

"No, I mean, how would he recognize Richard? Did he ever see him before his mission?"

Sister Pugh drew herself up, pulled a lace handkerchief from the front of her dress and waved floral scent in Megan's face. "Of course not! But I have seen him many times. I recognized the description. Our family is not stupid, my dear."

Unfortunately, information wasn't as available as anecdotes in which Richard often played only a minor role. She heard about the notorious legislator for whom Richard researched all night, only to have the legislator reverse his position the next morning. She heard about the couple Richard was going to teach the missionary lessons to, only to discover they'd joined the church five years before in Ohio.

After each conversation, Megan had another piece in her hand. But often she couldn't even tell if it belonged to the puzzle she hoped to solve, let alone how it connected with the other pieces. Sometimes she felt that something had been withheld from her. Almost always she closed the conversation feeling tinged by something like pity.

One morning she called the number for the graduate student from Murray and found he was working on a doctorate in the east. She looked at the other names and began dialing. The next one on her list had been from Hill Air Force Base. She called the base and found he had been transferred to Seoul, Korea. The next one lived in Boise, and someone at that number promised to have her call Megan back that evening. Megan looked at the last number. It was in someplace called Cow Spring, Arizona.

Suddenly she was exhausted. Laura Black, she whispered and pushed the numbers. Just make this call, she promised herself, and you can quit for today. The children would be knocking at the Gingerbread House door soon anyway. The phone on the other end of the line was ringing now, a faraway buzz that irritated her ear. It kept ringing.

As she moved the receiver to hang up, she heard a voice. "Hello? Hello?" Megan said.

"Yes, what is it?"

"Hello, I'm calling Laura Black. Is this Laura Black?"

She pressed the receiver close and blocked her other ear. She felt as if she had placed the call overseas, the connection was so fragmented. Also, the voice in her ear had a lilt — an accent?

"Laura who?"

"Laura Black. Is Laura Black there?"

"No. Who is this?"

"My name is Megan Stevens . . . " Her voice trailed off as she heard voices on the other end. Then she heard a brisk pounding like the keys on the cash registers she'd loved to watch as a child and, sure enough, the ding of a bell. The voice returned. "Sorry. Can't talk to you now. You'll have to call back."

"But is Laura there? Is a Laura Black there?"

With a burst of static the line went dead. Megan hung up slowly. Strange. Had the telephone been in a store? A gas station? Surely not a home. Where was Cow Spring, anyway? She would have to look it up in the atlas. But not now. Now she must walk into Gingerbread House to answer the knocking at the door.

"The trail is cold," she told Alan that night.

"Well, did you talk to all the researchers?"

"Yes. Not much there."

"How about all the grad students?"

She told him about her calls. "The woman in Boise called back, but she didn't have much to say. She said she didn't work with Richard often. She said she took all her questions to Sue or Jim."

"Let's call Cow Spring again," Alan said. "Nice name, isn't it."

Megan sighed and carried the living room extension close to the fireplace where Alan sprawled with his customary olive green pillow. "Where's the number, Meg?"

"I'll get it." But she didn't. Instead she buried her head in her hands and found her hands trembling. Her thoughts wobbled, too. She looked up, feeling desperate.

"It's not worth another long distance charge, Alan. Wherever that number reaches, nobody there is going to be any help. I've struck out and I'm sick of all this. I have too much else to do. Did I tell you the Girl Scouts are after me again to help with Elinor's group? They have to sell all those cookies, then go on a spring field trip. And Bucky's just home from the hospital after having his tonsils and adenoids out. I need to run the get well cards all of the children did over to him."

"What you need is a full-time detective," Alan drawled.

"Want to take that on?"

He shook his head. "I've got enough jobs."

"Listen, Alan, if you hadn't shown up today just in time for finger painting, I'm not sure what would have happened. I had to send Roxy home with that bad cough, and I knew Elinor wouldn't be home for hours."

"Things slowed down between therapy sessions," Alan shrugged, his way of dismissing her thanks, as if he loved squatting on small chairs among squirmy bodies. "Do I still have blue glop in my ear?"

"Let me see," Megan said, sliding closer on the

couch. Suddenly — no, again, for this was becoming a familiar impulse — she wanted her hands on his hair, his face, her lips against his ear. She slid away. They were friends. *She* was the one of uncertain status. Alan did so much for her and her children. It wasn't fair to keep adding roles. A detective now? Then what? She thought she felt her face unexpectedly blush.

"Where are the kids?" Alan asked. "The older ones."

"Bec's gone to bed. She headed in there right after school and has done nothing but sleep. I hope she isn't coming down with the flu. Scott's doing his homework."

"Why don't we run out for a while? I've been resisting a great Mexican pot I saw in the mall. You can talk me into buying it."

"Okay. Just let me check on everyone. I'll be ready in a few minutes."

———

Megan held the pot, running her fingers over its black, glossy surface, all the way to Alan's apartment. "It'll look beautiful on your coffee table," she said. "I love it."

He gave her his warm, brown glance. Tonight it heated her face. She held the pot closer. Her hair had grown wavy and full. She liked the way it slid about her neck, hiding her face when she bent forward. She thought she looked better than she had for years. At least, she felt better. If the improvement left Alan unmoved, that would be a little disappointing, though it made life simpler.

They set the pot on the table. "Wine to celebrate," Alan said, turning toward the kitchen. "Let's not tell anyone it's non-alcoholic."

"Does that satisfy your weekday or Sunday inhibitions, counselor?" Megan teased.

"Both," he smiled, pouring, "not to mention my ulcer." He handed her a glass filled three-quarters of the way. They drank. Then Megan set her glass on the coffee table beside the pot. "It's good," she said. The air grew peculiarly still, the floor fell under her feet as if she'd stepped into an elevator. She couldn't move her eyes from his. For just a second she didn't care what her eyes said. It was true.

"Come here," Alan pulled her close, and she lifted her face. They kissed, once, then again, reaching to hold, to touch. They looked at each other and laughed in relief and acknowledgement.

Snuggled beside him on the couch, she tardily remembered her resolve to keep his friendship. "Mmmm, nice," she said, lightly. Now he could draw back and reach for his glass, as if something pleasant, but nothing momentous, had happened. But he was still holding her. He bent again for her lips. With joy, she realized that he was more than reciprocating her desire. When they drew apart, she ran her hands up his taut arms, then opened her eyes a little to see his face over her, dark and stressed. Later she would remember the two of them as floating, her hand cupping his head, his face against her ear, locked in a long, hard embrace. She could almost believe that they each had found again something precious and perishable.

She was not gone long, but when Alan dropped her off at home she found Becky shaking in her bed, tears rolling on to the sheet she clutched in both hands. Scott had lined up water, juice, aspirin, and a thermometer on her nightstand and stood nearby literally wringing his hands.

Megan began doing everything at once, despite the tumult inside her. "Your fever is only 100," she said. "What is it, Becky? Where do you hurt?"

"My throat," Becky gasped. "My neck. My head. My side. I ache all over."

Megan put the heating pad under her, aspirin down her throat, and found some low music on the radio.

"Try to get some sleep, honey."

"I can't."

"Why not?"

"I have to go to the bathroom."

"Well, come on."

"I can't. I'm too tired, Mom. I'm exhausted."

Megan helped her out of bed. It was true, she could barely walk. "Tomorrow we're getting you to the doctor," she said. "Do you want me to sit up with you?"

"Just for a few minutes until I get to sleep."

But Megan sat in the chair beside Becky's bed most of the night, dozing off and on, dreaming of Alan. She recalled as precisely as possible every second at his apartment and squirmed in her chair as she felt her body respond again to his touch. Sleep and worry wound through the memories, for Becky slept lightly. Several times Megan woke to find her daughter curled around a pillow and whimpering.

For the next three weeks, Megan spent every possible minute with Becky, nursing her through the acute phase of mononucleosis. There were no magical pills or injections, just bed rest. But that meant bringing food and drink, hook-

ing up the extension to the telephone, wheeling in the por-
table television, and apply encouragement often, like a healing balm.

Megan felt she was paving a path between Gingerbread house and Becky's bedroom. She was homebound.
Yet the adrenalin of crisis and the excitement of what had
flared between her and Alan energized her. Alan came over
for late suppers after the children were settled at night. They
held each other while omelets set, kissed while steaks fried,
and talked endlessly, sprawled on the carpet, too tired to
move.

Then the crisis ended and real life began to crowd
in. Megan helped Becky with overdue homework and welcomed Heidi's visits more than Becky seemed to, but no
other friends came by. Megan also kept track of voluminous
cookie orders for Elinor, who turned out to be a champion
salesperson, and she agreed to drive troop members to
Montezuma Creek—if Becky recovered in time and if no
other driver could be found.

Sometime during those weeks, Megan made a tran-
sition. She could hardly remember wanting anything in quite
the way she wanted Alan. She asked nothing but to be with
him, and each time was a celebration. She loved him. If she
loved Richard still, and she wasn't sure she did, if had nothing to do with loving Alan. Loving Alan was like loving
spring sunshine.

As Becky recovered, Megan drove to Alan's apartment evenings when she could get away for a few hours.
When she drove home through Bountiful's sleeping streets,
she rolled her window down. She shivered but loved smell-

ing spring in the cold air. She felt suspended in a soaring song of praise.

But her sense of well-being only highlighted Becky's listlessness. One day after Elinor took over in Gingerbread House, Megan decided to try to bring Becky to life again. She brushed her hair to one side and clipped it in a ponytail. Once Becky would have scorned such a simple hairstyle, but now she shook her head almost tearfully when Megan suggested adding a ribbon. Megan led her into the bathroom and insisted she brush her teeth and wash her face.

"I had a bath last night," Becky mumbled around the toothpaste.

"I'll be right back," Megan said.

She went to her room and pulled out a pale pink bed jacket she'd never worn. Richard had given it to her after Heather was born, but it didn't button down the front so she couldn't nurse conveniently. By the time she was no longer nursing, she forgot about it.

She helped Becky into it. "Okay. Back into bed. Pretty soon you're going to start feeling like yourself again."

"Whoever that is," Becky said.

Megan sat down on the bed. "It must seem like a long time," she said.

"It's been an awfully long time since I went to a game or marched with the drill team," Becky said. "I haven't done that since before Christmas."

"You haven't? Why not? Were you feeling unwell even then?"

"No. I just decided it wasn't important. Not for me."

"But why, Becky? Was it breaking up with Court?"

Becky sighed. "Mom, have there been any calls for me while I've been sick that you haven't told me about? Has anyone else wanted to come and see me?"

"No, just Heidi. Then you know the girls in the ward came by to bring those flowers, and Kim called once."

"Not my seminary teacher or anyone like that?"

"I think the student secretary called once. Why?"

"Oh," Becky said, "I just thought Brother Leavitt might call."

Megan was surprised but tried not to show it. "I guess that's not too much to expect."

Becky smiled, but tears ran down her cheeks.

"Oh, honey, don't. He must be awfully busy."

"Yes," Becky said. "He must be." Her chin shook, then her cheeks. Becky covered her face and wept.

Megan gathered her in and waited.

"I was seeing a lot of him, Mom."

"Brother Leavitt?"

"Yes. He was teaching me about the way he lives. He said I was young and could be pure again."

"He said what?"

"Well, Court and I had messed around a little. Brother Leavitt was helping me repent. That's how it all started."

"How what started?" Megan heard her voice rise slightly.

"He gave this talk in class on purity, you know? And he looked right at me, and his eyes just burned into mine. I felt awful. So I went to his office after school late that day. I told him about Court, and he gave me a father's blessing — since Dad's gone."

Why didn't you come to me sooner, Megan wanted to cry, but she folded her hands, nodded, and kept still.

"I don't know, Mom, but when he touched me, put his hands on my head, I just felt it all the way through. Do you know what I mean?"

Megan nodded.

"So we kept talking. He told me about his wife, Ruthie. She's just perfect, Mom. So spiritual."

Becky was crying harder now, her tears crowding out the words. "Oh, honey," Megan said. "it's so natural to get a crush on someone like that. You could've told me."

Becky didn't stop crying, but now laughter was mixed with her sobs. Megan ran for an ice-cold washcloth and a glass of cold water. Becky took both and her hysteria quieted.

"See, Mom, a little later, *after* I knew I loved him, I found out about his wife Tami." Becky giggled, her face crumpled, but the words poured out. Megan's face felt frozen. "Then I found out about his wife, Katy . . . " Now Becky was hysterical, again, and Megan breathless with a desperate calm.

"Here," Megan said, "come on, Bec, drink this up. It's all right."

"He wouldn't risk it," Becky squeaked, pushing the glass away. "That's how much he loved me, Mom. He wouldn't risk calling."

By the time Alan came by that night, Becky was sleeping. Megan briefed him, her sentences efficient, and asked him to stay with her children. He agreed. He watched her as she checked the telephone book. "Meg," he said, "maybe we should all three talk about this."

Megan looked up from the tiny notebook where she was jotting down an address. "Later, Alan. Okay?" she said on her way out the door.

————————

As Megan drove, she felt her outrage flare into rage itself. Her foot trembled on the accelerator, and she pressed down a little harder. Her hands gripped the wheel until they felt melded to the plastic.

That beast! One mental picture replaced another as she imagined the last few months during which Becky had become so subdued, so well-scrubbed. She saw Becky waiting outside an office, Becky shaking a firm, warm hand much larger than her freckled one, Becky's adoring eyes turned upward to a face Megan could not visualize except for the confident, pious smile, Becky on her knees beside a figure in a suit, Becky closing her eyes for a kiss not quite a father's, and yet . . .

She wasn't even seventeen! And she was supposed to become this Brother Leavitt's wife? One wife, and no doubt she'd be pregnant before she was eighteen. Megan had married young, but not that young, and she and Richard had, at least, given themselves wholly to one another.

Pretty Becky, with her round blue eyes, curving cheeks and breasts and hips. Megan suddenly glimpsed her daughter pale and heavier, a baby on her hip, but her face still curved like a child's, lined up with other young women, more children, and one man beaming at them all from behind a wide-lens camera. Damn him!

Megan took the corner of into the subdivision fast, feeling dangerous. She'd fix this hypocrite. Even Richard, if Richard were here, could not be more enraged, or more effective. And if Richard was here with his daughter who was so quickly becoming a woman, would Becky be falling in love with her seminary teacher?

Megan was taking corners slower now, her eyes straining for house numbers and street signs. Whoever had designed the subdivision had planned so that no ray of artificial light would ever strike either side of a corner sign, she decided. And they'd succeeded; she was lost.

She pulled to the curb and shifted the car into park, then dropped her forehead to the cool steering wheel. She stretched and flexed her fingers. Abruptly, foolishness prickled over her, leaving her clammy. She stared out the windshield at the double row of houses, families who knew who they were and where they were going, not crazy people who roared around strange subdivisions ready to avenge the wrongs of history without even a decent sense of direction.

She should have brought Alan. She even could have called the bishop. This was, after all, a matter for the priesthood. A polygamist recruiting in the seminary was sinful stuff. But no, she'd rushed off so sure she could resolve everything. So here she sat, lost. And on this block or the next or the next her nemesis was praying with his wives, or tossing his children, or reading the scriptures in preparation for tomorrow's lesson. Her fury would probably choke her words, her threats, and he would smile and say something calm and lordly, and she would yell at him or weep. Suddenly Megan felt her nakedness under her clothes and missed her garments. Would he somehow know or see she wasn't wearing them?

She turned off the headlights, feeling as exposed and ridiculous as on the hot afternoon when she'd been stripping off her wet swimming suit after a shower bath outside. Unknowingly, her father had whipped open her bedroom door to introduce the daughter of a visiting client. She must have been about nine at the time, Megan thought. He had paused there, stunned, in his gray suit and tie that so perfectly matched his hair and eyes even in his late thirties, and behind him Megan saw a strange man look away and a girl, older than Megan, begin to smirk. All she could do was cross her arms in front of her body and bend a little.

Of course, he had apologized and shut the door, but eventually, dressed, she'd had to open it and play the hostess.

Megan's hands twisted in her lap. Maybe she should drive to a telephone and call someone. She could get directions at the same time. She rolled down her window halfway to get some night air. For a moment, the outside air seemed stale and still, but then a breeze floated in, brushed her face, and drifted through the car. Megan breathed deeply. Crickets were chanting vigorously in the hedges, she noticed; they'd adapted to her heartbeat.

She would not give in. Somehow, she would marshal her forces. Beyond the street, she could sense the valley, the marshes and foothills, then the mountains circling the sky's dome. She felt herself settle into the cosmos, a pinpoint, to be sure, but a definite one, something purposeful. She tried to pray but had the same odd sense she'd had before, praying about Richard, that she was imploring an ear that would listen most considerately but not really understand. So what could she draw on? Who would help her?

She thought of her mother, but carefully. Her mother almost always agreed with her father and her father would see this as a matter for the priesthood and the God who separated the true priesthood from the polygamists. But, still, if her mother knew about this — this affront to her granddaughter's innocence, to her future — Megan captured a jolt of indignation and quickly closed that door. She packed the indignation inside her with the outrage and felt her body warm and relax.

For another minute or two, she listened to the night and found within it the sense of a force quite different than the one she'd been trained to tug down from heaven. This force seeped up from the darkened earth like life itself and stirred quietly in the breeze, encompassing, enfolding, healing, and settling to rights. She'd felt it before in unsolicited moments of blessing.

She shifted gears and swung the car around at right angles to the nearest corner so that her high beams glared on the sign. She figured the street coordinates, got her bearings, backed up, waited for a pickup to pass, and made a U-turn. Then she drove to Leavitt's house as if it were a billboard she passed every day of her life.

Megan walked up the sidewalk in her crepe-soled

shoes without a sound, but her heels rang in her heart like bells. This was for Becky. This was for herself.

———————

A light-haired, pale woman in her twenties answered the door of the small brick-and-siding house. She wore a white blouse and a simple skirt. "Mrs. Leavitt?" Megan said, deliberately avoiding the title Sister.

"Yes."

"I need to see your husband, Boyd Leavitt. My name is Megan Stevens."

"Oh."

Megan thought she saw something flash in the young woman's eyes. "I'm afraid he isn't in right now."

"Then I'll wait until he comes home or you call him. May I come in?"

"Well . . . " The woman moved the door an inch toward Megan, but it was too late. Megan was halfway inside. She had never before been so pushy.

"I believe you know my daughter, Becky," she said, moving through the entry hall into the living room.

The woman said nothing, for now Megan could see that Boyd Leavitt stood there, his hands dangling at his sides. He was an ordinary looking man, average height, a full head of brown, wavy hair. Nothing like Richard.

Megan smiled. She felt dangerous. "I'm Megan Stevens. Becky's mother."

He held out his hand. She ignored it. "Won't you come in, Sister Stevens. Please sit down. I must apologize for my wife. I was working on tomorrow's lesson and asked not to be disturbed."

Megan walked across the living room's thin, tan carpet. She sat down on the green vinyl couch. She thought she had seen motel rooms more personally decorated. "Which wife?" Megan said pleasantly. "Is this Ruthie? Or Tami? Or Katy? Or maybe another's been added since Becky got so sick?"

There was a silence, which the woman broke so gently that Megan was almost ashamed. "I'm Ruth," she said, sitting down beside her husband. "How is Becky?"

"She'll recover. She was a little hurt that she didn't hear from you, Mr. Leavitt. I understand you declared your love rather enthusiastically when she was well."

Ruth looked at her hands. "We all love Becky," she managed.

"So I hear," said Megan. She continued looking at Leavitt.

"Sister Stevens, I can see that you're upset," he began, "but no one has intended Becky any harm. Indeed, we offered her our greatest trust — you must understand our need for caution when we are such a religious and civic minority. Now we offer that trust to you."

Ruth smiled at her.

"That would be a mistake," Megan said. "I suppose you have the right to your own way of life. But doesn't it strike you that recruiting among impressionable seminary students is pretty tacky?"

"Why? They are the youth of Zion, Sister Stevens."

"And they are brought up to see you as a priesthood leader. To trust you implicitly. Especially the vulnerable ones. The girls like Becky." Her voice sounded hard. She folded her trembling hands.

Anger flashed across the Leavitts' faces, but it was quickly gone.

"You don't understand," Ruth said. "We aren't evil."

"I have been commanded in this, as well as in teaching seminary," Leavitt said. "You must know that the most worthy girls are in those classes." He smiled at Ruth and patted her hand. Then his voice changed, and he lifted his hands, his fingers pointed upward. His eyebrows lifted as he looked Megan over. "Are you comfortable questioning the Lord's direction, Sister Stevens?"

Megan felt her anger rise hot and strong. She made her voice reasonable. "I suppose you have to find them young."

Ruth flushed. Megan suddenly wanted to apologize to her but didn't dare to show weakness. Ruth, not more than twenty-two, was the first wife. Megan had not seen any children, but toys were piled in one corner by the overstuffed chair.

Leavitt shifted his weight forward, touched his slightly graying temples. "You can ruin me," he said, staring hard at Megan's face.

"I doubt that," she said. "But I bet I can get you out of Bountiful High's seminary. This is your first year here, isn't it? When they ran you out of wherever you were before, I'm sure there were those who helped you."

"There were," he said, rising. "There are many of us, and we only gain strength in adversity. Think of your own conscience when you fight against the Lord's own truth."

"Good night, Ruth," Megan said. She stood and
walked to the door. Leavitt followed her. Just across the
threshold, an impulse struck her. She lifted and shook each
shoe in a gesture she had only read about before but knew
Boyd Leavitt would recognize.

Becky cried and laughed in Megan's arms when she
got back and reported on her visit. Alan said little. Megan
thought he looked at her oddly once or twice, as if he had
never seen her just that way before. She was surprised at the
hug he gave Becky before he left and doubly surprised that
Becky returned it so warmly. "Thanks, Alan," Becky said,
her voice catching. Then she buried her face in Megan's lap
and wept.

"I can find my way out," Alan said with a little
wave. Megan waved back with a victory sign.

The next day Becky listened gravely as Megan called
the seminary principal, then she took the telephone and spoke
with him herself.

"What do you think Brother Leavitt will do?" she
asked Megan later.

"He'll find someplace else. He'll probably move before
they can excommunicate him. I don't like being involved in
this at all, Bec. Still, I can't help but see him as a predator."

Becky nodded, but tears seeped from her eyes. She
closed them and leaned back on her pillow. "It's so funny,"
she said. "I feel half like I did when Court and I broke up,
and half the way I felt after Dad disappeared."

"I didn't give you much help either time, did I,
Becky?"

"Well, you did enough this time!" Becky burst out. "I know you meant well, Mom, but I'm always going to love him. I just know it. But I also know that he'll probably hate me the rest of his life."

Megan resisted saying, "Let's hope," and settled for shaking her head. She thought Becky was asleep by the time she found something to say. "Bec," she murmured into her daughter's damp hair, "do you think you could give up romance for a year or so and give us all a rest?"

Becky's blue eyes opened. "Could *you?*"

18

KRISTIN

I'm making you uncomfortable," Kristin said, dancing back
to the sofa from the stereo. He didn't look uncomfortable,
though, leaning back, hands under his blond head. His hair
looked gold in the lamp glow. It would turn white gracefully, probably without losing much of its fullness. Greg would
be good-looking for a long time yet.

"You're the one dancing around," he said. She sat
down and folded her hands. He always made her feel a little
rash, even though his eyes and words told her often how
attractive he found her. She loved his mannerly polish, as if
he were descended from a long line of sterling silver. His
family sounded ordinary enough, although she'd never met
his brothers and sister. His parents were dead.

"So you've been hanging out with those radical Salt
Lake and Provo women again," he said.

"Right. Real radicals. Temple-goers, every one of them, I bet. Well, maybe not Cheri or Suzanne. I don't know. They know so much, Greg. It's amazing. At least come to this lecture with me next week about the pioneer midwives. I think you'll enjoy it and it would be fun to discuss afterward."

"Over here," he called. She snuggled back into the crook of his arm, and he kissed her. "Maybe. Got to go now, love. I'm on call tonight."

"Too bad. I'll escort you to your car, doctor." She peeked in at the girls, watching the end of a television movie, and told them to get their baths once it ended. "I'll be back in a while. I'm going to Megan's."

She held Greg's hand while they walked to the car. She liked the feel of his hand, long and hard and dry. "You never sweat," she said suddenly.

"What?"

"Oh, nothing."

He kissed the tip of her nose. "I'll call you."

"Right. Bye, now."

Before his gray Porsche rounded the corner, Kristin was in her Volkswagen. Megan, she thought grimly, had better be home. Otherwise she'd go route her out of Alan's apartment. After all, Megan had been her friend first.

She could hardly wait to tell her how scandalized people were about Boyd Leavitt. He'd vanished from the seminary, and word had spread quickly. A polygamist! And a seminary teacher! People would talk about it for years.

Half the people Kristin had seen at the clinic—or at the ward—considered Megan a heroine. The rest, like Greg, just raised their eyebrows as if *naturally* the Stevens family would be mixed up in something unusual.

Still, Kristin thought starting the car, she had never heard polygamy discussed in a group without a twinkle in some man's eye. There was always the stalwart who had to remind everybody it was an eternal principle, something you'd have to reckon with in the hereafter. Pie in the sky, she muttered, backing out of her driveway.

When Kristin bounded into Megan's living room, she found Megan packing to take Elinor on a Girl Scout field trip. While Megan bustled in and out, shorts and socks in her arms, Elinor showed Kristin Montezuma Creek on the road map. Kristin had never even noticed that dot in the southeastern corner of the state.

"You're kidding," she said.

"It's in Navajo country," Elinor said solemnly. "We're going to an authentic pow wow."

"I see," Kristin said. "That's wonderful."

Megan bent over their shoulders. "Isn't that remote? And look down here, just over the Arizona border. Cow Spring. That's where one of Richard's graduate students came from."

"Really? But he'd never go back would he? Who'd want to live down there after getting an education?"

"It was a she," Megan said. "I don't know. I couldn't track her down. Maybe if we have time, Elinor and I will drive down there and ask around."

"Mmmm. That looks even smaller than Montezuma Creek," Kristin said. "I wonder who you'd ask. Cows?"

"Sheep," Elinor said seriously. "Navajos raise sheep. I don't know about cows."

"Terrific. Well, I hope you have a good time, Elinor. It looks like a real adventure."

"That's what we thought," Elinor beamed, then bent her white head over the map again.

Once Kristin got Megan in her car, she had a question that sounded more like a demand. "How did you get stuck with this field trip? I wouldn't drive a carful of kids down there if my honor depended on it."

"I thought I'd left myself a lot of loopholes. They just closed up at the last minute, that's all."

"Megan, anyone should be able to protect herself from a Girl Scout trip to Montezuma Creek. After all, you did help with the cookie drive. I thought I'd never get those stacks of boxes out of my living room, and one deadbeat ran out on Bonny, same as usual. That was enough civic service to hold me for another year."

"Well, I only said I'd help if they couldn't get anyone else. And if Becky felt better."

"You call those loopholes? I told them I'd drive if every other adult in the valley came down with the plague."

Megan laughed. "Well, you don't have Elinor to reckon with. Just when it looked as if I could get out of it, she brought me an article she copied in the school library. It was about how middle children tend to be overlooked."

"You're kidding! What a manipulator."

"No, she just thought she had a case. I guess she did, too."

"Mmmm." Kristin turned toward the canyon. "Well,

she helps you so much in Gingerbread House. I guess if anyone deserves an outing it's Elinor."

"True. It won't be so bad. We'll just go down first thing in the morning and come back the next day. I've heard it's a pretty drive if you take the Bicentennial Highway from Hanksville."

"Elinor showed me. That's got to add a good hour to the trip."

Megan sighed. "Well, I think I'm on Elinor's agenda. I might as well enjoy it."

There was a steady, hard bumping under the car. "Shoot," Kristin said, turning the wheel to the right and braking slowly. "We've got a blowout."

Megan was looking at her, her face alarmed.

"Hey, it's okay. I've got a spare."

"Oh, good. I was just thinking about all those miles on the highway with just Elinor. Would you believe I've never changed a tire?"

"Lucky you," Kristin said. "It's not a lot of fun. Let's talk a minute first." The front of the car overlooked Bountiful's slopes of street and porch lights, the dark fields across the tracks, the ghostly image of the lake beyond.

"You know, Meg, you're the talk of the town again," Kristin said. "It's almost as though someone flashed a neon sign reading BOYD LEAVITT, POLYGAMOUS SEMI-NARY TEACHER, EXPOSED BY MEGAN STEVENS. So to speak."

"Terrific. How did everybody find out?"

"The way everybody always does. Instantaneous com-munication. Somebody ought to patent it." As Megan shook her head, Kristin sobered. "I guess you didn't need this, though. How's Becky doing, really?"

"Pretty well. She's back in school full days now. Already there's a boy bringing her home."

"Who?" Kristin sighed and opened her door. Megan got out and followed her around to the trunk.

"His name is Brett. He seems nice enough. She hasn't said much about him." Kristin shook her head and settled the jack under the bumper. "To think I've got all that to look forward to with my girls. I can hardly survive it myself."

"So how is Greg?"

"Fine. Nice. Charming," Kristin said between pumps on the jack handle. "Now the lug nuts. Observe."

"So? About Greg, I mean. Here, let me do one."

The wheel off, Kristin sighed sharply. "I don't know, Megan. I care for him, but it just doesn't seem to go anywhere. You know what? We don't trust each other much."

"Trust is tough. Maybe it will get better. Maybe he's scared."

"Maybe. I am, for Bonny and Sheri's sake. Stepfathers are a risky business. My girls' nightmares and therapy are over. But I can't take any more risks with funny fathers."

"True," Megan said, and handed her the lug nuts, one by one.

Inside the car again, Megan asked, "Do you remember when we preserved flowers in Relief Society maybe eighteen months ago? We'd bury the petals in sand and dry them out until they were just colored dust."

"Really? I didn't see those, I guess."

"They were pretty, but they gave me the creeps. I didn't finish mine. I felt like a mortician. No, a mummifier." Kristin laughed. "Maybe I'm a mummifier for wanting things permanent. My kids can be mummies. Greg can be a mummy, too, in his operating room greens." She started the car. "Better get back."

Part way down the hill, Kristin put her foot on the brake, looked at Megan, then accelerated again. "Maybe that's not so funny. I still have Bryce propped up in the bedroom corner, don't I?"

Megan stared at her. "And how about you?" Kristin continued. "Isn't Richard still hiding under the pyracantha?"

They were almost back to Megan's house when she answered, "Maybe he is. He must wonder what's going on."

"Oh, Meg," Kristin heard herself say wistfully, "I won't ask if you're happy. You seem happy. But do you think it'll last?" She thought of the rumors beginning to circle the ward, rumors that Megan was seeing someone.

Megan was quiet a minute, then reached over and gave Kristin a hug. "I don't know. The feeling is more mellow now, not so sharp. I think I'll last. That's the difference. And I'm ready for anything."

"Including Montezuma Creek," Kristin said wryly. "Have fun!" She drove home. She kissed the girls, who were still awake in their beds and shut off the lights. She sat down in the dark living room and looked out the window into the shadows of the street. As if on cue, the telephone rang. It was Bryce.

"How's it going?" he said, in a voice so casual, so familiar that her heart caught.

"Fine, but I don't have time to talk."

"I want to see the girls."

"Come and visit."

"Kris. Come on, honey. I want to take them somewhere."

"No."

"Hey, I've been to all that court-ordered therapy. That's it, Kris. I did it, and the ball's in my court now." She could hear a sneer in his voice. She had never liked him angry. "I'll take *you* to court."

"I'll see you there. Bring your therapist with you."

She hung up. A minute later, the phone rang again. Kristin lifted the receiver, then let it down again without answering. "Daddy, Daddy, Daddy," the girls used to call when he came home from work. The sound still echoed in her head. She wondered if it did in theirs. And in his.

She thought about Greg and his efforts to please Bonny and Sheri. They liked him. But he was not their father.

It was quiet as she sat in the dark living room. She wished Bryce would drive over to talk about it. She knew she would never let him alone with them again without a fight.

Seeing him was a poignant fantasy, just the same, and she let it creep over her. Bryce would steal in the front door, sit down beside her in the dark without a word. After a while, they would talk and cry and hold each other, among the other dark shapes of the living room. They would let their past pass.

The canyon breeze huffed through the screen. Maybe

next week she'd adjust the glass panes in the door, but not now. A car braked down the street, and she closed her eyes, listening for approaching footsteps. But maybe it wasn't Bryce. Maybe, sitting here like a fool by a drafty, unlocked door, she was setting herself up. Any greasy, foul moron could pull off the freeway and drive down her street and find her here without a man.

Any man, parked in that armchair would be a deterrent, she thought, staring through the door defiantly. He could be stupid or ugly or mean — all the better to discourage the rabid stranger. A wimp in the armchair would be unfortunate, but even a wimp would mark her as somebody's, prove she was not fair game; she belonged.

Her breath caught. Stupid, stupid, she told herself. The breeze was downright cold now, and more persistent. She hadn't jogged; she'd better exercise. Let him come through the screen, whoever he was. The squeal of a knife against metal. She was ready — ready to kick him so hard he'd never get up again.

Outside, the crickets persisted, yet the breeze was becoming a wind. She wished for lightning, thunder, tornado, a torrent that lasted all night. She was stiff from sitting so still, and her head ached.

Minutes went by. Behind her clasped fingers, her locked eyelids, Kristin imagined herself old, lame with arthritis, her hips, knees, ankles aching bone deep. She was walking down the hall toward bed, leaning on the arm of a man. He was taller than she, even though he stooped a little with age.

"It's Greg," she whispered, but hadn't she already caught the gleam of the hall light on bronze hair?

Longing swept over her. She turned her face up to the wind, eyes still closed. Again she imagined the old couple, who had tugged and pushed one another through many crises, helping each other down the hall toward sleep.

Exercise, she told herself, and get to bed. But she stayed on the footstool by the door, listening for the wind through her tears.

MEGAN

They stopped for ice cream bars and gasoline in Hanksville. The town was comprised of a grocery store, a service station, and one long motel, huddling together in the rosy desert. By the time Megan turned the ignition key again and bit into cold vanilla sweetness, she felt as light-hearted as Elinor. The morning had started badly. As the girls shivered in their shorts outside the wardhouse at 5 a.m., the leaders had paced around tote bags and pillows trying to get organized.

"We figured five girls to a van and four in the station wagon," Lisa was saying. "But Mindy and Jeralee both have tonsillitis. In fact their whole family does. That brings us down two."

Megan's tongue itched to volunteer not to drive, but Elinor was holding fast to her hand and she could feel her excitement.

"Let's put four girls per vehicle," she suggested instead. But when they began dividing up the girls, the trouble began. Not only had they organized into groups of five, but no one wanted to ride in the station wagon. They all linked arms and fought to stay in their chosen groups. Elinor watched them with disdain.

"This is getting silly," Lisa said. "Choose a friend or two, Elinor." Megan's heart ached for her. Elinor and her peers were often on completely different wavelengths, but she was still sensitive to their snubs. Even Jody and Marcia, her best school friends, were lobbying to ride in the same van. "Just come with us, Elinor," Jody said a little shamefacedly.

Elinor lifted her chin. "Let them all go in the vans. My mom and I prefer to ride alone."

Everyone breathed a sigh of relief, and the girls cheered, abandoning any pretense of tact. "See you down there," Megan said brightly. After a quick prayer for the safety of the outing (to which Megan added her own postscript for Becky, Scott, and Heather at home), she and Elinor hopped into the car and were gone while the others still wrangled their belongings on to the vans.

A mile or two past Hanksville, Megan handed Elinor her empty ice cream stick. "Put that in the litter bag, will you? You know what? I don't think this highway is so spectacular. Pretty is all."

"Pink and green," Elinor agreed.

But around another turn or two, both gasped and Megan braked to slow their descent between towering red cliffs streaked with black, firs growing precipitously at improbable angles from any patch of dirt in a crevice.

"Wow," Elinor breathed, as they wound down the switchbacks, every view ahead breathtaking, and the cliffs to either side demanding their attention. "Look, Mom, five or six trolls are bunched up there, talking at the edge of the cliff. They look like people after church."

Megan looked at the knobby formations overlooking the highway and nodded. "Or maybe they're sentinels," she suggested. "Maybe it's an enchanted land?"

"Navajo country sounds magic," Elinor said. "But we aren't there yet. Maybe this part is troll country."

"Don't you think it was Navajo country once though? It looks like the postcards of Navajos herding sheep in the desert."

After they passed the red rock and the spectacular junction of the Dirty Devil and the Colorado Rivers, there was a long stretch of sage and juniper that seemed especially dull by contrast. Elinor's eyes blinked after the first few miles; she yawned. Soon she was asleep.

Megan welcomed the solitude. She had privately resolved to find some time for a walk, or half an hour to watch a sunset — time when she could think without interruption. She wanted to sort out her feelings about Alan. It was so easy to talk to him, to consult him, to take his advice. She was beginning to depend on him in a lot of ways, and that worried her.

"Relax," he said once. "You don't think I'll abandon you, do you?" But it wasn't that simple. She had been half of a whole for a long time, and she wanted time to become whole before she became half again. Officially, she was still married. But was she in any way free?

What's more, her parents would be coming home from their mission very soon. The mental picture of them walking through her front door filled her with panic. What would they think about their daughter now? Would they approve of the way she managed their finances and the children's problems? Worse, what about Megan's own changes? She had shed her garments like a symbol of all that had betrayed her, shut her out. Now did she want to move closer to the church? Might she marry Alan — or some-one else — in the temple? What would they think of Alan — or Kris? Would they feel she was married to Richard for-ever? And if they disapproved, whether they said so or not, was she prepared to handle that? Had she truly grown up?

She passed the turnoff to the Natural Arch National Monument. " 'Knowing how way leads on to way,' " she whispered, glancing at Elinor, but she still slept, looking intent as if her dreams absorbed her. The phrase repeated in Megan's mind. What did it come from? "Knowing how way leads on to way . . . I doubted that I should ever come back." Robert Frost. She had memorized the poem in high school and thought she would remember it forever. But now she only recalled bits, the first and last lines, and those two in the middle.

Her head ached lightly by the time Elinor opened her eyes then sat up straight. "Where are we? What did I miss?"

"Not a thing. We just got to the main highway. Let's

go up to Blanding for lunch and get our bearings. Then it's on to Indian country!"

They got a hamburger, then walked around town. "Look," Elinor breathed, as they approached a Navajo woman sitting on the sidewalk outside the post office. Her hair was bound at the nape of her neck, and her hands were busy with yarn in the lap of her gathered calico skirt.

Megan took Elinor's hand and they walked quickly to the car. "Back to the highway. We head south, then east," Megan told her. Anticipation rose in between her ribs as she turned the key. "Let's go! Elinor, do you know that poem by Robert Frost that starts 'Two roads diverged in a yellow wood'?"

" 'And knowing' . . , " Elinor said. "And knowing what?"

Trying to reconstruct the poem, they drove through the sleepy town of Bluff, then east to Montezuma Creek. The red rock gave way to low mesas. Here and there oil pumps rhythmically bit the earth. Blue and yellow wild flowers interspersed the sage, and Elinor spied another Navajo woman with a blue umbrella. She waved a stick at a flock of sheep and goats.

"Elinor, look way over there. See? Like a huge ant hill. Is that a hogan?" Now she could see the wooden door in the pink mound of clay. How do they live in there? she wondered. She hadn't felt so downright curious for a long time.

"You know, Monument Valley isn't that far from here, even though we'd have to double back. Let's drive through there before we go home," Megan smiled when Elinor clapped her hands.

"Wait until Scott hears about our trip," she gloated. "And the girls!" Megan felt a pang for her middle child, bent again over the road map.

When they reached Montezuma Creek, at first they saw only cars and vans, lots of them, parked all around the little town of trailers and small homes. "What a funny house," Elinor said, pointing at a frame, eight-sided house with glass windows and an air-conditioner on top. Megan parked the car, then looked where she pointed.

"Oh, I know," Elinor added. "It's a modern hogan."

"Really? How do you know?"

"Eight sides. See, there's another house like that, but not so fancy." They locked the car and followed a stream of people, mostly Navajo, toward a baseball field. They could hear drums now and a steady hum of voices. Megan couldn't catch the conversation around her, moved closer, and realized nearly everyone was speaking Navajo. No one met her eyes, but smiles flashed from one person to another like mirrors.

They found a shady spot to watch the pow wow, in between a pickup truck and one of a very few dusty-looking trees. There was room just for the two of them, Elinor tucked almost under Megan's arm. A cool breeze wound under the branches of the tree, and they were on the front lines, yet almost invisible. People, Indian and white, surged past them, glancing at them startled sometimes, once they were almost past.

"This is perfect," Elinor said. "The troop is over there, see? Out in the sun."

"Don't wave," Megan urged, "or we'll be out in the sun, too." She tried to absorb everything to tell her other children. She and Elinor had not left Utah, yet they were in a different world, one they'd never known existed. A group of Navajos approached and passed them. The men wore jeans, buttoned shirts and cowboy hats. Their string ties were clamped with turquoise. Turquoise brooches, rings, bracelets and earrings covered the women, some pieces so large that Megan wondered how heavy they were to wear. The women older than Megan wore bright gathered skirts and velvet blouses. Their legs were wrapped in white, their hair tied with white wool.

Three young boys in levis and running shoes brushed by them. "All from the valley," one sneered in English. "I can tell."

"How?" his friend asked. "I bet you can't. Your grandma looks just like them." The third boy giggled.

"I saw the pink dust in their hubcaps," the first said. Then they all laughed and said something in Navajo.

"Pink dust?" Elinor said wonderingly.

"From the red rock, I guess," Megan said. "Remember back by Bluff how red the earth was? The valley, he said. Maybe Monument Valley?"

"I bet you're right. We've got to go there. Oh, Mom look at that little girl!"

Megan and Elinor watched children parade their costumes. "Maybe the littlest ones will dance, too," Elinor wished.

Before long, the drums boomed in earnest, singers gathered around the drums, and dancers began stepping in a circle. For the first number or two, Megan concentrated hard on the steps, the dancers, what the meaning might be behind the dance. But eventually the drum matched her own heartbeat, the soles of her feet throbbed with the pulse of the earth under them, and she let her eyes wander freely. She felt a part of the impromptu, yet patterned, dance.

As the sun sank, people dropped too, sitting on blankets, cushions, folding chairs. The light softened. Little children played around the outskirts of the crowd, chasing each other while their parents gossiped with kin or watched the dances. Toddlers padded through the dust; here and there one crawled.

Megan thought the babies beautiful, with their triangular dark eyes, round cheeks, and glossy black hair. One wearing only a disposable diaper and a little yellow rosette in her hair caught her eye. The baby wasn't quite walking yet. There was something in the way she placed her hands and feet squarely on the ground, then looked around before trying to stand, that reminded Megan of Heather as a baby. Funny, the little characteristics you forget until you see them again, she thought.

The baby pushed herself up, then sat down hard, tipping over in the dust. A young woman came over and picked her up. She dusted her off, but the baby kicked to be free. Her mother, who wore jeans and a loose smock, shrugged and set her down.

The man on the pickup guffawed, and the woman smiled at him. "Hello, Charlie."

"How do you like Montezuma Creek?" he asked in English, his voice soft. The woman smiled. "We like it. The little one likes it the most. She has even more of my family here than back home by the springs. Maybe she will get spoiled."

The man chuckled. "But another one coming. That's good." Megan watched as the woman walked back to her place on the sidelines. She was pregnant again. Her hair hung down her back like a black curtain. She shrugged and said something to the white man standing next to her. He seemed to laugh, turning his head sideways. It was that twist of the head that froze Megan's eyes. She stared at him, but he obviously didn't feel it. Maybe she was mistaken. When he pulled the girl in with a tanned arm, and glanced back at the baby, she got her first full look at his face. Yes. It was Richard.

Megan took half a step back behind the tree's boughs and breathed deeply. Her heart was louder than the drums. She looked again at the baby, the chubby triangle, hands and feet on ground, so much like Heather. Swiftly, Megan counted, but she didn't need to. Her own baby would be just about that age now, had it been born.

In a whirl of intuition, she suddenly knew everything. Later she could think how she knew.

The drums, the dance went on. She could feel Elinor beside her, silent, brushing lightly against her. Megan wondered if she'd seen her father, but didn't dare ask. She watched as Richard and the woman turned away to talk with an older couple—the baby's grandparents? She watched as her own legs stepped forward and stooped beside the baby with the yellow rosette. She saw her own extended hands.

The black eyes looked at hers, and she saw how they tilted at the corners. Like Scott's. Like Richard's. Megan smiled. The baby held out her arms. In one motion, Megan lifted her and stood, her eyes checking to see that Richard and the woman had not turned back. Still smiling, she stepped back by the tree, ready to shrug and speak to any onlooker. But the man by the truck was looking for something inside the cab. She waited a few seconds, before she moved back through the crowd. Her free hand snatched the yellow rosette from the baby's hair and put it in her jeans pocket. Behind her, she knew, a dozen Navajo babies played in the dust. It would take an hour to check with all the relatives and friends who might pick Richard's baby up. By that time, Megan might have brought her back.

She walked swiftly, Elinor at her side, jiggling the baby as if they played a game. She opened the car door and plopped the baby on Elinor's lap. Fortunately, they were not hemmed in. Ahead of them there was just enough space to snake around the elementary school, then through the playground to the road.

She didn't speak until they reached the highway. She could hear Elinor murmuring to the baby. She drove fast, although she knew it would be a while before anyone called who? Indian police? A sheriff?

"Elinor," she said then, "I haven't the faintest idea how to explain this to you."

Two pair of eyes, one black and one pale blue looked

back at her. "Explain what?" Elinor said. "I know what you're doing. You're bringing him home."

Megan saw a break in the traffic and took it. They would drive straight for Price, then Salt Lake. Monument Valley would have to wait. She smiled. "You're exactly right," she said and began to hum.

———————

All the way home, she felt she was fueling the car with her own energy. Nothing was a problem. She stopped for disposable diapers, a plastic bottle, a carton of milk, a box of crackers. Thoughts marched through her mind, orderly and logical, as if she had planned this random event for months. Vengeance is mine, she thought. Richard could not dismiss them now — unless he could ignore this baby as easily as he had ignored five of hers.

She intended to wait two weeks before contacting Richard: just the right amount of time for guilt, grief, and anger to totally replace the first numbing shock. Elinor had dubbed the baby Pooky. Don't tell anyone where Pooky came from until your father comes for her, Megan said, and Elinor promised.

"She's just on loan," Elinor told her siblings lightly when they startled Scott and Becky by arriving home just before midnight. "Her parents are coming to get her soon."

Megan knew that explanation wouldn't satisfy for long, but she still felt invincible. Her humiliation, her rejection, her disgrace, her stigma had been mobilized into action. A black-eyed baby was bringing her justice after all.

Her senses were alert, cautious, determined. She knew she couldn't risk making Kristin or Alan an accessory to a crime. She would trade Richard crime for crime, but she must not involve her friends.

She didn't sleep. She watched Pooky snore peacefully beside her. The few minutes she had rocked Pooky, sweet in a pink nightgown Heather had worn, had infused her arms with memory and her heart with loss.

She thought about Pooky's mother, the woman who had lived by the springs. Cow Spring, Arizona. She remembered the odd dread that had stopped her from calling there a second time, the exhaustion that overwhelmed her.

How had this Laura Black fallen in love with Richard? Why had he gotten her pregnant? How could he leave his family and the home they had made for such a strange land? What would a Navajo girl see in blue-eyed, quick-talking Richard? How could she steal a married man from his family?

She had no answers, but she remembered how quiet Richard had been the first part of the year and his mood swings around Christmas. When had he decided to leave them? Had he ever considered telling her he had fathered someone else's child? What would she have done?

She could let Richard wait two weeks. She, after all, had lived more than a year with an uncertainty that was hell. But Pooky was a baby. The memory of her mother in a loose smock kept Megan awake. That woman took Richard away, she argued. Together, they took my baby and wrecked our lives. But her anger was past now, fulfilled and vanished like a mushroom cloud.

Dawn lightened the sky outside her Priscilla curtains when she got wearily out of bed. There was something she had to do. She looked back at Pooky's round little body under the sheet. You should have been mine, she thought. Then knowing her mother was searching and crying somewhere in a land of beauty and desolation, she went to the desk and typed a note to Richard in care of the post office in Montezuma Creek. She told herself she was giving in because there would be too many complications if Pooky stayed more than a very few days. But she knew she could not cause another woman to suffer week after week, month after month, as she had suffered.

When she returned to bed, the room was nearly light, but the baby still slept. Megan kissed her index finger and touched the baby's head lightly. She slid under the blanket and fell immediately asleep. In her dream she was driving home from Montezuma Creek with her children and Richard in the station wagon. Richard was talking and talking, telling them everything.

RICHARD

By the time he had left, his mourning was all done. Never
again, he thought, would he endure such a winter. Yet
now it was spring, and pain had doubled him again, for his
daughter had disappeared. It was not the same wrenching
loss as before, but a sudden body blow, a kick to the groin.

Last year Richard's anguish had seemed a part of
January's and February's stinging snow and hostile freezes.
The night before leaving home he'd lain in bed aching everywhere, as if he had been flayed alive. Bits of him clung to
Megan, Scott, all of them, everything. If only he could explain
why he must leave. But he had decided early he would spare
them that and keep his turmoil to himself.

He congratulated himself for that restraint, as well
as the courage to do what must be done.

Once on the road in the middle of March, Richard
turned giddy driving southeast in the old Ford Laura's friend

had loaned him. Richard's spirit skimmed the freeway as he realized that his plan to begin a new life was actually going to work.

He counted it as affirmation when later, weary from the ride, red rock and blue sky engulfed him. Leaves burst like spontaneous combustion. He rolled down the window and smiled.

Between Bluff and Mexican Hat, he sang. Laura would meet him at the cafe. He'd known enough to want her with him before he went on the reservation. Even so, he hadn't anticipated how foreign a country he had chosen as a haven, a retreat from his comfortable neighborhood that had turned stale.

Now the reservation was home, but where was their baby? He picked up beer cans as he walked toward the post office thinking how when you came to the reservation you changed time as well as place. Oh, there were aluminum cans to recycle and video games, but you picked up your own mail here and telephones were uncommon and unreliable.

"Here you go, Richard," said Larry Benally, handing him another can from the asphalt. Richard looked up, startled. Larry and his brothers were students in his social studies class. "Thanks, Larry," he said gravely, seeing that the empty can was a gesture of sympathy. Larry and his brothers nodded and walked past. Richard had once explained to everyone who caught him gathering cans that it wasn't the cash he cared about but just getting the cans off the street. After a few averted black eyes, he realized they took it as a criticism not camaraderie. Cash for cans they understood.

He'd stopped asking people if they'd seen his baby. They all knew Elena in town. They all knew Richard and Laura, even though they'd only moved from Cow Spring less than a year ago. He'd been certified as a teacher in college. With his experience in government and his willingness to start on the bottom rung of the pay salary, he found a job fairly easily once they moved to Montezuma Creek with its public high school. They parked the trailer in the court by the Texaco station, and they were settled.

How could Elena disappear in such a simple town where everyone is known? Richard wondered. Of course strangers had come to the pow wow. But approached by a stranger, wouldn't she scream? Wouldn't someone hear or see? He and Laura had been standing only a few feet away. A skinwalker did this, he had heard Laura's stepmother whisper, or a Navajo witch.

Richard sat down on a bench outside the post office, his elbows on his knees. He couldn't face going in yet. Just saying hello to Clark, behind the counter, who'd shake his head to show nothing had been discovered about their baby, accepting their mail and hoping, fearing some clue required him to catch his breath first.

He ached numbly everywhere. A couple of days after he left Megan, he remembered, he'd felt like this. Shocked to the core. Laura had a brother, Jimmy, Scott's age, and Richard had flinched every time he saw him. Laura thought he didn't like Jimmy hanging around. There wasn't much privacy in the complex of trailers, a frame house, and a cou-

ple of hogans a few miles into the back country outside of
Cow Spring. He'd tried to explain about Scott, and her eyes
flared with anger.

"Go home then!" she'd yelled, and he'd left the trailer
saying unnecessarily, "I'll be back." He'd glanced over his
shoulder once to see Laura's mother rustling over to the
trailer in her violet skirt. She could only visit her daughter
when he was not at home, the first Navajo custom he'd
learned and one he welcomed.

He'd set off for Cow Spring, the chilly wind in his
face. The trading post was about all there was in Cow Spring
and Richard decided they'd have to move and move soon.
He was too conspicuous here, and there was no place he
could work. What did people do out here for money? As he
expected, the trading post had a telephone. He started plug-
ging in quarters and dialed home. He heard Megan's voice
and knew she was intact. She hadn't had a breakdown or
driven off a canyon road. Of course not. He'd known all
along that Megan was strong. And Nancy was there. That
meant Meg was getting support from the ward.

He walked back feeling a touch of self pity. He would
be the bad guy back in Bountiful, he knew. People would be
noncommittal at first, but they would blame him sooner or
later. Even Laura didn't realize the extent of his sacrifice.
He'd left everything to Megan. Of course, she'd be hurt and
worried, but she could keep her unimpaired view of their
life together.

He hadn't been lucky enough to keep his view of
their marriage intact. He'd been sadly disillusioned about a
love he had assumed was strong and real half his life. Yet all

the weeks he had suffered, Megan had not even known. She had asked what was wrong. Working too hard, he'd say, a headache. *You* seem tired. I didn't want to bother you, he'd turn the conversation.

But did she ever press for more? Did she insist on access to his painfully double heart? She never said, "It must be more than that. You're in such pain." The fact that she did not in some way bolstered him; he soothed his aching nerves with a little of that indifference.

Finally there was the fact that he couldn't desert Laura, just twenty-one, with a child. His child. He couldn't face Megan, pregnant herself, with his dilemma. Not that Laura would ever give up her baby.

And Megan had four children already. She had friends, she was bright and experienced. She would be fine. It was Laura, who was alone and shy and who needed him. She was bright, too, the brightest of the graduate students once you broke through the reticence, but so young. Also, he admitted, he just couldn't give Laura up, and if he told Megan — no matter what they decided to do — he would have to say goodby. Imagining that scene turned him nauseous. Laura, whose little hands touched him everywhere, who demanded and entreated with never a word — no, he couldn't let go. She gave herself so wholly, like an unwrapped birthday present. Even the thought of her evoked the smell of her hair. Along his fingertips, he could sense the exact texture of her skin.

He bent from the waist, put both hands flat on the cool clay to stretch his back, then resumed walking. It was the vulnerability under Laura's competency that had won

him initially. He liked the way she wore her hair, straight
and black, not permed or streaked like so many Hispanic or
Indian young people. Her tailored shirts and skirts were
often set off by small turquoise earrings or a silver bracelet,
and she wore a large silver ring with a green turquoise on
the smooth, brown skin of her right hand. He liked that,
too. Because she was so quiet, he went out of his way to be
friendly. Just when he noticed how he liked meeting her
eyes, liked the nearness of their hands as they turned the
pages of legislative documents, he found that she did, too.
They were perfectly in sync.

Their love began as a mild excitement, a heightened
interest. Those mornings he had gone to work humming,
wondering whether a look, the brush of a hand or shoulder
or a chance to share lunch would happen today. Within
weeks he was coming home tense and tired. He'd find himself staring and muttering, For Becky, don't do it. For Elinor,
don't. Megan, Nutmeg, Raven, I won't, I promise. But it
turned out to be not unlike skiing, his favorite sport in college, something he'd given up after he married. Once you're
at the top of the hill, how unreasonable to do anything but
swoop down. A little way at least. Just to the first jump, the
third pine. Only one more run.

Then the exhilaration of Laura's returned love had
carried him through Christmas and New Year's. He couldn't
remember ever having been so happy, and it spilled over at
home and at church. Love, he was convinced, made everything harmonious and whole. Their love must be right and
beautiful. A giveaway, Laura had said, explaining the term.
She never asked about Megan, never wanted to hear about

his kids. She made him want to talk, she was so reticent. But he didn't.

The trailers were in sight now, and he leaned against a juniper fence to gather his thoughts and give Laura's mother the chance to leave.

He watched her raise her umbrella like a parasol against the sun and hustle toward her hogan, her purple skirts rippling. She said nothing, but he caught the hard glance from her black eyes like a rap on the brow. She was Laura's father's second wife, he'd learned yesterday. His first wife lived in Montezuma Creek.

"Maybe we could live there," Laura had said, when he told her Cow Spring might be awkward.

"Near your father's divorced wife?" he said.

Laura had smiled. "I didn't say divorced."

Polygamy wasn't common among Navajos any more, he'd learned, but it hadn't entirely disappeared either, especially among the older generations. Maybe that was why she'd introduced so many brothers and sisters who had turned out to be first cousins.

He hadn't met Laura's father, but he already envied him. Secrecy and deception were wrong, he thought, scraping pink mud off his boots on to an equally pink rock. The love wasn't wrong, but how society distorted things.

Society imposed rules and guilt that had made him realize he could no longer love Laura Friday afternoon, then rock Megan through their familiar ritual Saturday night, then substitute teach Scott's deacon's quorum Sunday morning. He felt divided. Laura's solemn news, then Megan's more casual announcement simply illustrated the schism in his heart. He imagined himself straddling a widening chasm like a ridiculous cartoon character — who never fell until he looked down.

By the first of February he and Laura had to make plans. She would return to her parents' home in Cow Spring, then he would join her. But everything contrived to make him stay: an assignment from the elders' quorum, Megan's birthday, the children's illnesses. Plus there were so many details to work out so he wouldn't get caught and so he wouldn't leave Megan in a bind. Laura had to be patient. Megan, of course, could not appreciate that.

Finally that Monday morning he had wakened knowing everything would fall into place, and it had. He knew where to leave his keys, how quickly to dress in order to leave enough time to say a silent goodbye to his family, one by one. His attache case, packed with his leather-working tools, a few papers, pictures of the family, a duplicate prescription of pills for his migraine headaches. He tried to think of everything. He'd read newspaper stories before where it seemed like guys had just disappeared. Some were found. He tried to remember what things had tripped them up. He made sure he'd have cash at the start. After that, he could manage.

———————

"Your wife — she needs you."

Richard jumped. Laura's father, Ben, lowered himself on to the steps at his side. Richard nodded.

"I know, Ben. Just came to check the mail."

"She's sitting by that window, one hand on her belly. May's there with her now. Been there all day."

"I appreciate that," Richard said. "You know, Ben, when I came here I found out that Laura could do just fine without me. I didn't know she had so much family."

Ben grunted.

"Of course I wanted to come," Richard added. "But still — you sure take care of each other."

"Get your mail, Rick," Ben said. "I told you she needs you. She's got one baby lost and another one kicking."

Richard sighed and stood up. "Maybe later we ought to take another look around the mesas."

"I'll go." Ben squinted up into the sun behind Richard. "I'll go south this time."

Richard nodded and opened the post office door. How had he ended up with such complications? He felt increasingly old.

He nodded at Clark behind the post office counter. "Morning, Rick." Clark handed him two utility bills and a small brown package. He stuck the bills in his back pocket and began unwrapping the package on his way out. Ben was gone. Too bad. Richard could have used his pocket knife. He still couldn't remember to carry one. The package was securely taped, and he leaned against a pickup while he worked at it. Inside he found a small, used can of nutmeg.

He stared at it for a full minute, then began to tremble. He looked back at the brown paper and found a white page folded into small squares. With shaking fingers, he unfolded it.

Bigamy is a crime. Child support for four children adds up. Richard, it's time to come home.

A chilly breeze from the direction of Red Mesa finally moved him. He folded the paper and put it in his pocket. He held the nutmeg nervously in his hand. He walked into the elementary school and asked to use the telephone. Maybe it was a trick. Until he found out, he couldn't risk telling anyone. But he had a little time; the Navajo Tribal Police wouldn't check back for a while, and the San Juan County Sheriff's department was just keeping the file open.

Waiting for a body, Richard thought. The telephone rang in his ear.

"Megan?"

"No, this is Becky. Who's this?"

Richard paused. His head hurt. "Is your mother there?" he muttered. "Just a minute. She's in Gingerbread House. I'll get her." Bec sounded puzzled as if she couldn't quite place his voice. He wasn't surprised. The connection was ragged and his voice sounded strange even to him. What had she said? Making a gingerbread house? He suddenly imagined Scott's scout troop or Elinor's Girl Scouts. Maybe the gingerbread house was for Relief Society. But hadn't she said Megan was *in* a gingerbread house?

As if he were lost and looking for directions, he unfolded the note and re-read it. He stopped when he came to the part about four children.

"Hello?"

He swallowed. "Megan."

Silence. He tried again. "Megan?"

"Hello, Richard. I thought you might call."

Her voice was confident, maybe ironic. "Megan. Is she there?"

"We're all here, Richard. You're the one who's missing." Then she gave in. Her voice softened. "Yes, she's here. She's fine."

He felt suddenly as if he was drowning. His eyes, nose, mouth all filled with fluid. He squeezed tears out of his eyes, sniffed hard, then cleared his throat, swallowed. "I just can't believe you did this," he said.

"Damn you, Richard! She's been gone two days. You've been gone more than a year. Don't you think we went through a little trauma when you didn't bother to come home one night?"

"About that . . . " He took a long breath, cleared his throat. "The note says four children. What . . . ?"

"I lost a baby, too, Richard. I don't suppose you can give it back." Richard took the phone away from his ear and stared at it. His hand was shaking. He suddenly remembered a bad dream of nuclear war, everything chaotic, uncontrollable. He put the telephone back against his ear. "I'm sorry, Megan."

"I'm hanging up, Richard. If you want her, come and get her!" The line went dead.

He'd almost reached the trailer when he felt his brain click into action. It was clear that Megan was in control. He could accuse her of kidnapping, but probably she would only get her hands slapped. Some smart lawyer would just say that Richard had abandoned his family, married again, and falsified his Social Security number. He hadn't paid back the loan. This could cost him and Laura a fortune. It would be a mess. He could deal with Megan himself, he didn't want lawyers involved. *One* thing about Megan. He knew his baby was safe, and that was what he'd tell Laura.

"You can't go back there!" Laura said. She was standing by the tiny kitchen sink, tears of relief and rage still on her face. "I'm calling the sheriff, Rick. He can go get Laney and put that baby-snatcher in jail."

"No," Richard said. "Listen, honey. She can put me in jail for abandoning them, for failure to pay child support. I don't know what all. Don't you see that we've got to be careful?"

"You're not going back." She turned away, but not before he saw something else in her face. It shocked him.

"Laura? Look at me."

He took her in his arms, turned up her chin. She was pale with fear. "Wait a minute," Richard said, "I'm just going to get our baby. You're not worried?"

She pushed out of his arms like Becky used to in a fit of anger. "Oh, no, I'm not worried! You're the man who can walk out the door and leave his family. What am I supposed to think?"

"No," Richard said. "I'm going to get our baby. I'm coming back." But she wouldn't look him in the eye after that, and when they went to bed right after a halfhearted dinner of hot dogs and beans, she turned away. He could only curl against her back if he wanted comfort before tomorrow's confrontation.

At dawn Richard woke from a dream of Becky as a curly-headed baby. He was tossing her in the air. His hands tingled from the swish of ruffles against his hands when he caught her again and again. She'd been wearing that pink frothy thing Megan dressed her in on Sundays. In the dream it had never occurred to him he might miss, fail to catch her. What if he had? he thought now.

He rolled over with the sated feeling of someone who has fasted, then eaten too much. Trying to fall asleep again, he realized he had not asked Megan how their children were. The griping in his guts headed him toward the tiny bathroom and told him what he should have known as soon as he unwrapped that nutmeg. Going home was going to be harder than leaving.

21

MEGAN

Megan warmed the pink lotion on her hands and watched Alan pace from one end of the living room to the other. Pooky, naked and plump, grinned at her in anticipation as she carefully slid her slick fingers beneath the baby's double chin. Uneasy the first time, Pooky now loved being rubbed with lotion before she was put to bed.

"I just can't believe you did it!" Alan said again.

"That's what Richard said. Do you think I ever believed that he could abandon us? And remarry? And start a family?"

"But Megan," Alan said, "you, of all people, taking a baby!"

Megan sighed and kept rubbing. How she loved the sensuousness of a baby, the smell of Ivory soap and Johnson's baby shampoo. She smoothed the creases in Pooky's tan legs with lotion, then bent and kissed her nose so that Pooky laughed and grabbed Megan's hair. Megan freed herself and turned the baby onto her stomach. Pooky poked her black head up and babbled at Alan. He looked at her but was too upset to smile.

"Alan, remember, I didn't want to tell you. You practically browbeat it out of me. I didn't want you involved."

"Didn't want me involved? If it's you committing a *crime*, how can I not be involved?"

"Alan, I'm responsible. I know why I did it and I know what I'm doing now."

"And you do know it was wrong?"

Megan bent and kissed Pooky's soft hair. "Yes, but you forget. Richard and his woman took my baby, too."

"I know, Meg." His voice softened. He sat down, then jumped up again. "But that doesn't make it right."

"Whoops," Megan said, grabbing the end of the towel Pooky lay on. She soaked up the growing wetness under the baby. "Well, now maybe you'll keep this diaper dry for a while." She turned Pooky over on to a dry diaper, rolling the wet towel into a ball she tossed it on to the ad section of the newspaper.

"I can see it all now," Alan said, trying to get some humor back in his voice. "You're falling in love with that kid, and Richard's not going to let you keep her."

"I know." She snapped Pooky into a sleepsuit and picked her up for a big hug and a deep breath — the full effect of sweetness. "Who would have thought it? She just feels so good."

Alan plopped down beside them on the couch. "I'm

sorry I yelled. It's just that I care about you. I don't want anything else bad to happen to you. And I respect you, too. I *expect* you to . . . "

"To do what you want me to," Megan finished for him, fighting back a smile but feeling her eyebrows lift.

Alan closed his mouth with a snap and sagged back on the couch. "Okay, I'm out of line. Do you want to tell me about it? Have you told Kristin?"

"No, I haven't told Kris. For one thing, she's flat in bed with the flu. But after Richard comes to get Pooky, I'm going to descend on Kristin with some chicken soup and tell her the whole story. I can't wait to see what she thinks about it. Do you think she'll yell at me, too?"

Megan left the room without waiting for an answer. She put Pooky into an old travel crib she'd set up in her bedroom. Her neck and shoulder felt slightly damp where the baby had nestled, a familiar sensation that scratched the heart.

She went into the kitchen. "Come out here, Alan," she called. "I'll fix us a strawberry drink. Maybe I should add 7-up for your stomach?"

He came out and perched on a stool. Now he would listen. She told him about Montezuma Creek, about the lovely young woman with a curtain of black hair, about the baby who reminded her of Heather, and about Richard.

"I wrote to Richard that very night, Alan. Actually, early the next morning, but I hadn't slept. He'll be here tomorrow. And I have an attorney now. He's drawing up some papers, but he gave me a rough outline to give Richard.

He said he doesn't expect Richard to make much trouble and that I should be able to keep the house."

"I should hope so. You won't press charges for desertion or bigamy?"

"No, but it's an implicit threat I guess. What good would it do? It'd hurt us all. If Richard will cooperate in the settlement and custody, I'll trade him kidnapping for his crimes."

Alan was silent. She brought him a tall, pink drink and looked in the cupboard for plastic straws. When she brought him the straw, he put his arm around her.

"Why did you do it this way?"

"I've been trying to figure that out, too. At the moment, when I saw Richard and the woman and the baby, I knew what to do and I did it. I've not been sorry I did, although I know it caused pain. You're right. In a way, it's wrong. But in another way, a way that answers whatever prompted me that day, it's right."

She sipped the drink lovingly. Nothing spoke of spring quite like strawberries.

"I think I did it because Richard defeated us by not telling us he was leaving and why. He left us with such terrible questions. Somehow I had to make him confront us. Talking to him, sending him a letter . . . what good would it do? I had to really get him . . . get his attention."

"I'll bet you did get his attention," Alan said, and they both laughed, easing the tension a little. "She's a lovely baby," Alan added.

"Funny," Megan said, "but that little bundle asleep

in there is the cause of everything and she doesn't even know it."

Alan said nothing, just held her in his look.

"Oh, she's not the cause really, just an effect. But still. Both of us must have been pregnant at the same time." She giggled. "Poor Richard." She laughed again. "How can I laugh about it?" she asked, and wiped her eyes. "Damn him."

"You told the kids?" Alan asked. "If you like, I'll help explain . . . "

"Yes, I already did. You should have come a little earlier to get in on that." At his wince, she said, "Just as well. They took it like little soldiers. I don't know how they'll do tomorrow when he comes."

"How about you?" He still sat on the stool. All evening he'd seemed to hold her away from him. The balance between them had shifted, Megan realized. "How am I?" She wanted to dance, sigh, smile, shout and stomp all at once. "I think I need to go for a walk. Want to come?"

She went to Becky's room and asked her to listen for Pooky, picked up a sweater, then slipped out the front door with Alan. They walked until their legs ached, talking little. Back by Alan's car parked in the driveway, she stood on tiptoe and kissed him lightly. "Alan," she began, then lost her place, looking at him.

He smiled. He pulled her against him and held her that way for a long time. She could hear his heart beating, fast and steady as if it would never stop. But she didn't believe that any more. Everything was fragile, yet nothing ended. She wanted to kiss him, to thank him, but instead

she held him and let him hold her. By the next time she saw
him, Richard would have come and gone. She had never
thought beyond that event.

"Good night, Alan," she said at last, then nuzzled
into his shoulder again to blink back surprising tears. She
watched him get into his car and drive away. For a moment
she felt like a lost child, then resolution filled her full and
solid. No, she was fine.

She looked down the street, up at the cloud-splotched
sky, watched the dark trees twitter their newborn leaves.
Good night, night, she whispered, and ducked into her lighted
house. Richard was late. Megan fretted and paced while
Pooky and Heather played peacefully in Gingerbread House
with the children. She pictured him sitting in a car just
around the corner, trying to gather his nerve. She wanted to
go looking for him, but of course she couldn't leave.

When she heard a noisy muffler, then squeaky brakes
outside, it took her a minute to react. Richard had always
kept their car perfectly in tune. She went to the living room
window and looked out. An old blue sedan was parked in
front of the house, and Richard, looking pale despite his tan
and sun-bleached hair, was walking kiddy-corner across the
lawn. She stood and watched, framing the moment like a
photograph. Even when she could no longer see him, she
waited to know if he would ring the bell. He did.

Megan closed her eyes and took a deep breath. Letting it out slowly, she walked to the door, wiping her sweaty
palms on the sides of her white slacks. She opened the door,
then stepped back. Neither of them quite looked at the other.

But then he was inside and they stood there, the two

of them, where they had so often paused to say hello or goodby without any particular significance.

"How was the ride?" she heard her voice say.

"Fine. Is she all right?"

"I'll get her."

Megan walked through the kitchen to Gingerbread House and opened the laundry room door before she realized Richard was a few steps behind her. Had he always moved that quietly? He looked over her shoulder into the playroom, where the children were whirling and skipping to Mozart. Heather was circling with them, hands locked around Pooky's belly.

She felt Richard sag against the door frame.

"Are you all right?"

"Yes." His voice was tight. "Do you know what hell the last few days have been since I've seen her?"

"I think so." Her voice cracked. She tried to turn it to ice, not tears. "Of course it's been more than a year since you've seen Heather." She swallowed hard. "She's the one in overalls. Recognize her?"

But the children had seen them in the doorway. Pooky took two steps toward them before she dropped to all fours. Heather stared. As Richard stooped to sweep up the baby, Heather turned her back and bent over, poised bottom up, one arm extended, as the melody stopped.

Megan pushed Richard, his face buried in Pooky's neck, toward the kitchen. "It's time to send the children home," she said. "I'll be right back."

At least she could spare Heather and herself any more of this tearful reunion.

A few minutes later, she and Heather walked into the living room hand in hand. Richard and Pooky sat together on the sofa. Megan had dressed Pooky in a little yellow dress Heather had once worn and placed the yellow rosette back in her hair.

Richard set Pooky on her feet. "Hi, Heather."

"Hi," she said in a small voice, but she held on to Megan's hand. Megan sat down in the rocking chair, Heather on her lap, as she heard the door open. "In here, Elinor," she called.

Elinor came in with Scott right behind her, breathing a little hard. He must have run all the way from junior high, Megan thought. They sat down, looking nervous and embarrassed as Richard said hello. Pooky dropped to all fours and crawled at full speed over to Elinor, who picked her up.

"We've been calling your other daughter Pooky," Elinor said in her clear, high voice. "I hope you aren't offended."

Richard's eyes flicked from Pooky to Elinor then around at the rest of them, as if he was unable to take them all in at once. Megan felt herself trembling. She wondered if they all were. Richard's mouth twitched. "Her name is Elena," he told Elinor in a voice that quavered.

"How do you spell it? It sounds like my name," Elinor said.

He told her. There was a silence as the baby waved her hands at her father, then made a dive for Elinor's shoe-laces.

Scott looked out the window as a car door slammed.

"Here's Bec, Dad," he said. Megan thought he sounded grateful that he'd found something to say.

"Okay, son."

They all looked toward the door, but it was a full
minute before Becky appeared. Then she stood, framed in
sunlight from the open door, staring at her father. "Brett's
waiting," she said, "my boyfriend. I just wanted to say hello,
Dad." She said it lightly, but her voice was hoarse.

Richard seemed transfixed.

"Becky, come and sit down," Megan said.

"I can't."

Megan looked hard at her. Becky sighed and perched
on the edge of a dining room chair. But her lifted elbows,
her glances toward the open door, all indicated that she was
poised for flight.

"I told the children where you've been living," Megan
said, then was cross at herself for helping Richard out. But
Scott was white, and Becky fragile. Surely Richard must
have found something to say to them all, some way to make
amends.

"It's very pretty down that way," Richard said politely,
as if small talk would see him through this, and then he
could leave. "There's more time there, somehow. More air,
more sky . . . " His voice faded into the general silence.
The children looked at one another, then back at Richard.

"You didn't say goodby," Heather blurted. She darted
across the room and grabbed Richard's knee. Awkwardly,
he lifted her and set her there. Her legs dangled. Her sisters
glared at her. Scott looked down at his hands and hunched
his shoulders.

"Actually, I did say goodby," Richard told her. "But you were asleep."

"That doesn't count. It's a rule to tell people when you're leaving and when you'll be back," Elinor said solemnly. "You always made us do that."

"I know," Richard said. He took out a red bandanna handkerchief and wiped his face. Megan found herself staring at it, trying to imagine it with his favorite gray suit that she sold at the yard sale.

"I don't expect you to understand or forgive me, Elinor," Richard was saying, "but I found myself in an impossible situation. I didn't want to hurt your feelings, but sometimes you just have to start over. You know, try again."

"Like a carving?" Scott asked suddenly. He almost smiled. "What are you carving, Daddy?" Heather asked, patting his shirt.

"Not exactly a carving," Richard said. He looked back at Scott hard, as if he were really seeing him for the first time. "Scott, you've grown!"

"What you mean is you wanted a new family, not us," Becky said. Her voice shook. "It's pretty obvious."

Richard shook his head helplessly. "No, you're oversimplifying, Bec. I still loved you. And I always thought I'd see you again. Maybe you'd come to visit."

"How could we?" Becky asked.

There was a silence, and in it, a tap on a horn.

"I'll make it up to you, Bec, somehow."

Becky shook her head and stood.

"Wait," Megan said. Richard would let Becky go

and nothing would be settled. He would be off the hook, but Becky wouldn't. "Richard!"

He lifted both arms stiffly and took a step toward his firstborn, but she shook her head violently, tears flying into the bright air, and ran. The storm door hissed. When it clicked shut, they all looked disappointed. "Go after her!" Megan said. "She needs you." They heard tires squeal and then a motor roared with a surge of gasoline. Richard raised his hands helplessly and sat down.

Megan covered her face. Why didn't he jump in that dumpy car and follow? Didn't he know that every time a boy or man touched Bec she hungered for her father's embrace?

She looked back at Richard. He was checking his watch. She heard Elinor's high voice. "Where's Elena?" she asked, slapping her knees. Elena didn't respond.

"Now we've done it," Megan said through her aching throat. "She doesn't know her own name."

"Where's Pooky?" Elinor asked. The baby chuckled, putting her hands on her own fat cheeks.

"Pooky probably means something terrible in Navajo," Richard said, and the children laughed. Hearing her father's voice, Pooky crawled back and claimed Richard's other knee. He juggled the baby and Heather awkwardly.

Megan had a sudden flash of Richard cradling baby Becky in his arms. Suddenly, she felt despair. She shouldn't have brought him back, shouldn't have let the children see how unnecessary they had become.

"Really," Richard said, sounding more confident, "I've missed all of you. Your mother and I will work this out. Sometime you can come down for vacation. How would that be? There are ruins to see and a lot of people have horses."

"Horses?" Heather said, bouncing on his knee. Elinor twisted her braid uncertainly and looked at Megan.

"I'd like to, Dad," Scott said. "I can go back with you right now. School's practically out anyway."

Megan could see that he meant it. "Not for several weeks," she said, and Scott glowered.

"How about now, Dad?"

Richard shifted uneasily. "You ought to finish school." Megan could see Richard didn't want to take him. Surely Scott could tell. But it was equally obvious that Scott was determined not to let Richard out of his sight.

Scott turned to her. How well she knew those light eyes, the tilt in the shoulders. "I wouldn't miss anything, would I, Mom?"

Megan swallowed hard.

"Now, son, don't pressure your mother," Richard said. Scott's eyes didn't move from her face. He wanted his father.

"So it's Pooky," Richard was saying to Heather and Elinor, reaching for the baby as if Scott's subject was closed.

Megan met Scott's eyes, a long look. A crease ran between his brows, as if he were years and years older. Megan pressed her fingers to her temples, then folded her hands in her lap.

"Richard, Scott would like to go back with you," Megan said. "He could finish the school year there, couldn't he?" Her fingers twisted. How could she let him go?

"I guess so. But it's not a good situation. You have to remember that Pooky's been missing for most of a week."

They stared at him stonily, then Elinor whooped. All of them began to laugh and couldn't stop. From squinted, tear-filled eyes, Megan saw Richard's face turn a dull red. He tried to join them, nervously, then choked and walked to the window, staring out, his back to them. "A week!" Elinor sputtered, starting them again. Even Heather seemed to understand the irony.

Scott stopped laughing first. "That's enough," he said. "I've got to get packed. Right, Dad?"

Richard, sullen beside the window, shrugged and sent a steely look to Megan.

Megan caught her breath. "Get cool clothes and your basketball and whatever else you think you'll need, Scott. I have some legal papers to give your dad."

Scott grinned at her then left. Elinor and Heather began putting Pooky through her "point-to" tricks. A little frantically, Megan thought.

Megan went to Richard's old desk and got the papers. "Let's sit down, Richard." They pulled up chairs at the dining room table. "These are preliminary, but they'll give you and your lawyer the general idea. Basically, you can sign these or contest."

He looked through them, his hands moving like an expert's, the way they did when he brought paperwork home from the legislature.

"You're sure this is what you want?" Richard said, "a divorce?"

"What are the options, Richard? You want to just come and go as you please?"

Richard sighed. "I'm not going to fight you on anything." He set the papers aside as if there were nothing to discuss.

"About Scott," he said. "Megan, I can't take him down there. Laura won't have it. You'll have to explain that to Scott, just that . . . "

"If you walk—or run—out that door without him, I'll call the police," Megan said. "There's a detective who'd be interested to change your missing person status." They glared at each other.

"There's a county sheriff looking for Elena," Richard said.

"So she's found. Case closed. My lord, Richard, Scott's your son. Maybe you'll have another one in a few months, but Scott's missed you terribly."

Richard nodded. "I've missed him. All of you. But . . . "

Megan interrupted. "Moving on is one thing, Richard. Cutting out—starting over, as you call it—is something else. You can't do it. Not really. So take these papers and get an attorney. You do have a job?"

"Yes."

"Good. And you'll take Scott for a while. Then maybe someone else."

"And what is it you have going on in the shop? You tend children?"

"Oh, Gingerbread House. A pre-school. In the fall I have a grant to start my master's degree. I'm going to specialize in teaching learning disabled pre-schoolers. Identify them early, help them get ready for school."

He nodded slowly, smiled. He looked at her, and in that minute she found him again. Her Richard. He lifted a hand and ran it over the back of her hair. "I like your hair longer. You look great."

Time jerked and stalled. She almost said, "You should have seen me ten months ago," but instead said, "You look . . . different. The sun, I guess."

"You've no idea how I've missed you, Meg," he said in a rush. The hand on her hair tightened. He drew her close. "And the kids. I'm sorry about the baby," he said into her ear. She put a hand on his shirt, felt the edge of his garments beneath it. She closed her eyes. For the length of one deep breath, her world was restored, seamless, and secure.

Then she pushed on that hand, detached herself, pulled back her chair and stood. Sure enough, Elinor and Heather stood side by side, watching.

"Run and see if Scott's ready," she said.

"Go on, Heather," Elinor instructed, "I'm watching Pooky." But Scott was rushing down the hall, his backpack on his shoulders. " 'Bye, Elinor, goodby, Heather. I'll send you postcards."

Scott stopped beside Megan and put an arm around her. He was almost her height, Megan noticed. He kissed her cheek. " 'Bye, Mom. I'm all set, but I need my allowance. Tell Bec to write."

"Dad's got your allowance for you," Megan said levelly. She wouldn't let herself obey her impulse to empty her wallet into his hands.

Now everything rushed. Already Scott had a hand
on the doorknob. "Write," she said. "We love you. We'll all
miss you." She filled her eyes with her son. He looked so
happy. She feared for him, but she knew if she let him go,
he'd come back.

Then Richard stood beside her, Pooky over his shoulder, the papers in his hand. It was all going so fast.

"Wait," she said, and stretched to kiss Pooky's dark
head before Richard could whisk her and Scott away, into
the yellow afternoon.

After they left, Megan went limp. She looked at the
girls, who seemed suddenly leggy. "Do you want to play
pencils?" Elinor was asking Heather.

"You'll let me?"

"You're getting older," Elinor said. "I'd better teach
you before I give it up altogether."

Megan filched a hug from each. When the girls were
gone to their room, Megan sank into the rocking chair and
looked around. The room seemed to vibrate with unsaid
words. She sat and rocked until the air felt as still as it
looked.

In the meantime, the afternoon sun turned the room
hazy. Spring was truly here now with no turning back. Dust
danced in the sunlight, sparkling, vanishing, tracking air
currents Megan could barely perceive. The chair arm under
her fingers felt sticky. She inspected it and found smudges
and tiny dents where Pooky had chewed on it. Who else
had cut teeth that way on their old coffee table? Becky?
Elinor?

Suddenly the room seemed full of marks and prints, smeared and overlapped, a detective's heyday. Invisible footprints marched toward and away from the front door. Richard's. Scott's. Kristin's. Becky's. Alan's. She had washed the picture window only that morning, yet she sensed that it was opaque with the invisible marks of small, pressed hands, noses smudged against the glass, even an occasional curious tongue. They were—all of them—so often peering out to see whoever seemed late arriving.

Sunlight flooded the room. Everywhere in this house, Megan understood, were her own prints, like a potter's hands on clay. Even if her touch was forgotten, it became imprinted. Everyone's did. Now distracted, now intent, they all went on shaping by sun and dusk what never seemed quite ready for the kiln.